Praise fc
THE CANDY BUMBER

Besides Lucius D. Clay, it is Gail S. Halvorsen who has undoubtedly become etched into the collective memory of all the Berliners. To me and my personal impression, he has been a great player on our way to freedom and democracy, even more than John F. Kennedy and his saying: "Ich bin ein Berliner" (I am a Berliner).

As a small nipper in 1948, I lived with my parents in one of the outlying suburbs of Berlin. As did every lad in Berlin, I knew all the types of aircraft that landed at minute intervals, and all the ones landing on the Havel River. To my chagrin, I never was a lucky winner, getting one of Gail's little parachutes with sweets. And I could not go to the airport because the walk and trip to Tempelhof was too far, and my parents could not be persuaded to let me go by myself. But news of these parachutes was the talk of the town.

The pilot Halvorsen and his crew were the reasons all of us began to call the airplanes "Rosinen Bombers" (Raisin Bombers) and changed the Berlin Airlift from a strategic exertion to sustain West Berlin, a part of the city and millions of people during the Blockade, to something much bigger. Those little parachutes demonstrated an act of humanity and were surely the starting point of the emotional attachment between the people of Berlin and the Americans.

Gail S. Halvorsen has been honored in many ways. He is part of the "political inventory" of the city, and underlined his love for Berlin with uncountable visits. Being the US Air Force Commander in Berlin-Tempelhof for a number of years—and it has not been a long time that there was held a plebiscite regarding the future of this historical airport, Tempelhof—I am sure he would have voted to keep the field intact and functioning. For sure we can say, "He is a Berliner."

His book will come at the perfect time. I am not only thinking of the 70th anniversary of the start of the Berlin Airlift, but of his upcoming 97th birthday. The Berlin Airlift was the beginning of the conciliation of Germany with former western enemies and their shared values—values that, since the beginning of this century, seem to have crumbled slightly.

So the remembrance of men like Gail S. Halvorsen and his endeavors for the German-American and European-American relationships is so very important, not only for the ample knowledge of history but also for a demand for political action here and today. The values shared through these stories are very current issues.

—Eberhard Diepgen
Governing Mayor of Berlin from 1984-1989 and 1991-2001

Few individuals become an icon during their own lifetime. And even fewer come from a more humble background, to be honored and respected by citizens of a foreign city, generals, politicians, and even by American presidents alike.

Gail Seymour Halvorsen is just such a man. It was not the words of a GI airman, nor the promises of a politician, that moved him to simply drop candy to the needy children of Berlin, during the famous Berlin Airlift of 1948-1949. It was a gesture of a humanitarian and the fulfillment of his Christian beliefs that moved Gail to disregard official military regulations and provide the countless children of Berlin something that had been lost during the years of war... hope.

Hope came not from the candy itself, but from the realization that someone cared enough to make the parachutes, to buy the sweets, and even risk his career for such a modest gesture.

During all the years of his long life, Gail never asserted fame unto himself. Rather, he always proclaimed he was just one of the pilots that did his job. He was part of the largest humanitarian airlift in history, using the small fragile C-54 cargo planes to prevent Soviet aggression from starting a war, save Berlin from East German communist rule, and keep the possibility open for a unified Germany.

The airlift, which provided food, fuel and employment for 2 million West Berliners, was extremely important, and included all the discomfort and hardships that a cold winter, hunger and lack of housing brought with it.

Gail Halvorsen's actions were only the smallest story of a huge undertaking. Yet the hope they inspired brought forth the endurance needed by both nations for the Airlift to succeed—and, ultimately, preserve a free Berlin.

After fighting a long, bitter war, the Americans wondered if the West Berlin citizens would hold out. On the other hand, the Germans could not believe that a former enemy would be so concerned about their well-being and future as to indulge in such an airlift. Gail Halvorsen would exemplify this trust by caring for the weakest members of German society: the children. The children that would become Germany's future.

I've met Gail Halvorsen many times over the years; first in 1978, during an air show on Rhein-Main Air Base, and watched as a strong middle-aged man from Berlin broke into tears, as he was introduced to a pilot, that had dropped him candy during that airlift.

Next, I watched as President Bill Clinton and German Chancellor Helmut Kohl closed Tempelhof Air Base in 1994, with Gail standing next to them on stage. In 2010, during the Air Force Ball on Ramstein Air Base, Commanding General William Ward interrupted his speech to salute the simple man, who was entering a side door after a delayed flight. A few years later, when President Obama was commemorating the 50th anniversary of Kennedy's speech on the steps of the Brandenburg Gate, the first man he mentioned from the audience was Gail.

But despite these respects paid by world leaders, it was the countless children whose schools he visited and whose minds he motivated, that meant much more to him. Just as soldiers and airmen of many ages have been inspired by his story, so will be the readers of this book. And hopefully, Gail's story of hope will put his same warm smile into your hearts.

We, from the Luftbrücke Frankfurt-Berlin 1948-1949 eingetragener Vereinare (Airlift Frankfurt-Berlin 1948-1949 registered associations) are proud to be part of the continuing, inspiring life story of Col. Gail Halvorsen, for future generations.

—Dr. Lutz Raettig
President, Luftbrücke Frankfurt–Berlin 1948–1949 e.V.
Managing Director, Morgan Stanley

—Dr. John Provan
Vice President, Luftbrücke Frankfurt–Berlin 1948–1949 e.V.
Military Historian

Gail Halvorsen is truly one of the greatest of the "Greatest Generation." His legacy of healing and hope will continue to be an inspiration for generations to come.

—Deidre Henderson
Senator, Utah State Senate

THE
CANDY
BOMBER

Untold Stories of the Berlin Airlift's Uncle Wiggly Wings

THE
CANDY
BOMBER

Untold Stories of the Berlin Airlift's Uncle Wiggly Wings

Gail S. Halvorsen
Denise H. Williams

Horizon Publishers
An imprint of Cedar Fort, Inc.
Springville, Utah

ISBN 13: 978-1-4621-3751-0

Published by Horizon Publishers, an imprint of Cedar Fort, Inc.
2373 W. 700 S., Springville, UT 84663
Distributed by Cedar Fort, Inc., www.cedarfort.com

Library of Congress Control Number: 2017954590

Cover design by Jeff Harvey and Shawnda T. Craig
Interior Design by M. Shaun McMurdie and Shawnda T. Craig
Cover design © 2017 by Cedar Fort, Inc.
Edited by Jessica Pettit and Jessica Romrell

Photos courtesy of
    Dennis Lyman
    Gail S. Halvorsen Family
    Gail Halvorsen Collection, L. Tom Perry Special Collections, Harold B. Lee Library, Brigham Young University, Provo, Utah
    James R. Stewart, executive director, Gail S. Halvorsen Aviation Education Foundation
    Paul J. Jensen, vice director, Gail S. Halvorsen Aviation Education Foundation
    Trish Griffee Photography

Printed in the United States of America

10 9 8 7 6 5 4 3 2 1

Printed on acid-free paper

We express our deep gratitude to Cedar Fort Publishing—thanks to Jessica Pettit, Elicia Cheney and Jessica Romrell, editors; Jeff Harvey, cover design; Shawnda Craig and Shaun McMurdie, interior design; and Mike Gee.

Without our friends at Brigham Young University Special Collections—Tom Wells, John Murphy, Lynn Clayton, Cindy Brightenburg, and staff—this book would not have been possible. They continue to collect, house, and share the Halvorsen Papers and Photos.

The Frankfurt-Berlin 1948-1949 Luftbrücke Association e.V., Tim Chopp and the Berlin Airlift Historical Foundation, James Stewart and the Halvorsen Aviation Education Foundation, and the Berlin Airlift Veterans Association are constant in their efforts to share the story of the Berlin Airlift, to teach it to children, and to remember those many individuals who did so much to make it happen. Thank you for all you do and have done for the Halvorsen family.

Thanks to Mercedes Simon Wild, for filling in more details about your experience as a child during the Berlin Airlift. Your tireless work has made a difference and you are part of our family.

Finally, thank you to those family members who came before us, for beloved children and grandchildren, and other loved ones to come after.

To Gail's wife Alta and children, Brad, Denise, Marilyn, Bob, Mike, and their wonderful spouses; to Denise's husband David; to our cherished grandchildren and great grandchildren; to Lorraine; to the 31 American and 39 British pilots and crew who lost their lives during the Airlift; and to young people everywhere who have hopes for a better world.

—Gail

CONTENTS

INTRODUCTION 1

PART 1: Before Becoming the Candy Bomber 5

Chapter One: Early Years 7

    Gail's Birth and First Years (1920-25) 7

    Our First Rigby Home (1925-27) 8

    Our Second Rigby Home (1927-34) 10

    The Cowboy Pilot Sparks My Passion for Flight 13

    My First Lesson in the Joy of Service 13

    Noticing My Mother's Sacrifice 14

Chapter Two: Life in Utah 17

    Jack Rich's Ranch (1934-36) 17

    A Heartbreaking Loss 19

    My Father and the Bit of the Horse 21

    Sugar Beets, Sports, and Work on the Garland Farm (1936-41) 21

    Lorraine Pace 25

Chapter Three: Born to Fly 27

    Looking Up 27

    My Flight Scholarship, Pilot License, and CAP Wings (1940-41) 29

    Losing a Friend to War 31

War and Military Pilot Training (1941–42) 32

Utah State and Alta Jolley (1942–43)............................33

Assigned to Active Duty, Earning my RAF and

    Army/Air Corp Wings (1943–46) 35

Brazil and the South Atlantic Theatre (1944–46) 39

Refusing a Command...41

Forteleza and the Amazon....................................42

Why I Stayed in the Military after the War....................43

PART 2: Becoming the Candy Bomber **55**

Chapter Four: The Berlin Airlift *57*

Volunteering for the Airlift 57

A Change of Heart 59

A Sightseeing Trip to Berlin and Meeting the Children........63

Little Decisions and Two Sticks of Gum 67

Chapter Five: Children of Berlin *77*

Uncle Wiggly Wings..77

A Firm Pact of Secrecy 80

Fog and the Mountain of Mail for Me 83

Just One More Drop..84

Operation Little Vittles....................................85

The Miracle of the Returned Silk Parachutes.................87

Parachute Donations.......................................88

Dropping Candy in East Berlin 91

A Special Christmas Eve 93

Hospital visits.. 93

Chapter Six: The Impact of Operation Little Vittles **105**

A Berlin Father's Birthday Gift..................................... 105

The Good Luck Teddy Bear.. 105

Mercedes and the Chickens.. 106

Peter Zimmerman.. 108

Klaus Rickowski 109

Passing the Torch 110

Reflections on the Heroes of the Berlin Airlift.................. 110

PART 3: The Candy Bomber Legacy............................... **123**

Chapter Seven: After the Berlin Airlift................................. **125**

Post Airlift Celebrations 125

Engagement, Marriage, and University of Florida.............. 126

My Work in Research and Development (1952-62)............... 129

Return to Germany (1962-65).......................................132

Back in the States (1965-68) 133

1969 Tempelhof Open House and Parachute Drop.............134

Chapter Eight: The Move to Berlin *143*

The New Commander (1970–74) 143

Four Years in Berlin 144

Meeting Mercedes 147

Leaving Berlin 149

Retirement (1974) 150

Chapter Nine: A Lifetime of Service *169*

Berlin–Utah Student Exchange Program 169

40th Anniversary of the Airlift 169

The Spirit of Freedom 170

50th Anniversary of the Airlift:

1998 *Spirit of Freedom* 69-Day European Tour 171

A Tribute to Alta and Lorraine 172

Without Hope, the Soul Dies 173

Hope Is the Name of the Game 174

EPILOGUE 193

APPENDIX 195

Gail's Dead Sea Saying 195

Lessons Learned from the Best Teachers 195

Honors and Awards 198

INTRODUCTION

Gail Seymour Halvorsen's life is the story of a humble Utah farm boy's love of flying, his love of freedom and service to his country, and his capacity for deep gratitude and service before self. Over his lifetime of more than 96 years, he has represented his country, the Airlifters, and his faith, around the world. As an educator and statesman of the highest caliber, he has inspired generations of young people to serve others and remember that it is the little decisions that set them on the course of life.

After earning his private pilot wings in 1941 and his Royal Air Force and Army Air Corps wings in 1944, Halvorsen served as C-47 and C-54 foreign transport pilot in the south Atlantic theater. After the war and during his volunteer service as pilot in the Berlin Airlift, he initiated "Operation Little Vittles." With his buddies' help in 1948–49, they dropped twenty tons of chocolate on parachutes to the children of West and East Berlin. They distributed three more tons to Berlin children's hospitals to those who couldn't go outside (*Gail Halvorsen Personal History, 1985*). This simple, self-initiated act inspired hope and was a catalyst to change bitter feelings to positive ones between countries embattled and embittered by war. The recognition he later received opened doors for him to spread his message of hope, attitude, gratitude, service before self, and "out of small things proceedeth that which is great" (*Doctrine and Covenants* 64:33). "The importance of small kind acts of service cannot immediately become evident," Halvorsen believes (Gail S. Halvorsen Interview, Denise Williams, July 2017).

Following his Airlift service, the Air Force sent Halvorsen to the University of Florida for his bachelor's and master's degrees in aeronautical engineering. He then served as a project engineer for cargo aircraft research and development in Ohio and Utah. In 1957 he was assigned to the Air Command and Staff College at Maxwell AFB, Alabama. Next, in California, he played a key role at the Air Force Space Systems Division, spending four years in the research and development of space vehicles, particularly the Titan III Space Launch vehicle. The Titan III was designed to launch the Dyna-Soar Lifting Body spacecraft and other military satellites into orbit (Gail S. Halvorsen Interview, Denise Williams, July

2017; Gail S. Halvorsen *Personal History, 1985;*.

Halvorsen next served in Wiesbaden and Frankfurt, West Germany from 1962–65 with the Foreign Technology division of Air Force Systems Command. Following his service in West Germany, he was assigned to the Pentagon in research and development for space and technology, where he helped develop plans for the advanced manned reusable spacecraft. In 1968 he was given command of the Vandenberg Air Force Base tracking station in California, which was involved in both satellite launch and orbit operations around the world.

From 1970–74 he was the commander of Tempelhof Air Base in Berlin, Germany—the very base he flew into in 1948! As commander of Tempelhof, he represented the US Air Force in Berlin. He was awarded the German Service Cross to the Order of Merit by a representative of Willy Brandt, President of Germany, for his service there.

He retired in 1974 after thirty-one years of service and about 7,000 flying hours. After his retirement from the military, he helped set up a student exchange program in 1980 called the Airlift of Understanding, a high school student exchange program between the state of Utah and the city of Berlin. He also served at Brigham Young University for ten years as Assistant Dean of Student Life (Gail S. Halvorsen, Interview, Denise Williams, July 2017; Alta Jolley History, Denise Williams, 2011).

He and his wife, Alta Jolley, have five children, twenty-four grandchildren, and fifty-three great grandchildren. They served three separate missions for their church, in Salt Lake City, England, and Russia.

A recipient of numerous awards and recognitions, Halvorsen continues his daily positive small acts of kindness and goodwill, lifting others by teaching about the Berlin Airlift and lessons learned in his life (Airlift/Tanker Association, Nov 1, 1999 post).

PART 1

BEFORE BECOMING
THE CANDY BOMBER

My Dad, along with his good friend Jess Earl, bought one of the very first horse-drawn wheat combines sold in northern Utah to work the fields near Wheelon.

Chapter One: Early Years

Gail's Birth and First Years (1920–25)

I was born in the Salt Lake City Holy Cross Hospital on October 10, 1920, to Luella Spencer Halvorsen and Basil Knudt Halvorsen. We lived on a little farm in Wheelon Canyon, located on the divide between Box Elder County and Cache County where the Bear river crosses near Fielding, Utah. Dad brought Mom down to Salt lake City for my delivery. I was the second child, joining my brother Sherman who was five years older than me. Seven years later my sister Marilyn was born.

My Dad, along with Jess Earl, a good friend, had bought one of the very first horse drawn wheat combines sold in northern Utah to work the fields near Wheelon. Stationary threshing machines had been used up to that time. We lived in Wheelon just a short time before moving to Draper, Utah to run a dairy farm.

The dairy farm was a failure and to get his money out, Dad had to trade it for a partial payment on a farm north of Rigby, Idaho. I remember the day we left Draper in the spring of 1925. We had a wagon loaded with all our belongings which we towed behind our old Model T Ford. I remember all of us singing, "Oh Utah, Oh Utah We Bid Thee Farewell, We're Going to the Sagebrush of Idaho to Dwell." Mom cried a little. She liked Utah.

Our First Rigby Home
(1925–27)

The farm in Idaho was by a small canal. I used to get excited when the irrigation water came in because we would find trout coming down from the Snake River through the canal into the irrigation ditches and out on the field. We would walk around collecting them to take into the house for dinner. In the winter we skated on it. Dad showed me how to skate when I was five.

The spring of 1926 we had a great flood that came down from the Snake River. Bishop O.J. Call, our neighbor, had warned us to leave the place. Dad carried his pet calf on his back up a ladder to the top of the haystack. He tied the calf to a stake and stayed behind putting things up high and freeing the cattle. Mom drove the Model T down the road just ahead of the flood. It was scary. I was afraid that Dad wouldn't be able to get across the water to where we were. Finally he joined us and I remember all of our neighbors sleeping together in the church that night.

That summer my brother and I walked into a field that had our big Jersey bull. Suddenly we saw him charge us from across the way. We turned and ran as fast as we could and just as he was about to gore us we came to the bank of the canal

One of my primary role models growing up was my brother Sherman, who was five years older than me.

and jumped and swam across just in time to escape. The water had been let out of the canal and I could touch bottom in most places or we might not have made it.

It was while we lived here that I remember my first lie. My cousins, Sherman and Thelma Perkins, from Stockton, California were visiting. Sherman and I were six years old and Thelma was just a few years younger. They wanted to go swimming in the irrigation ditch, but I knew that I had better ask Dad. I went clear out to the other end of the farm to find him and when I did he said no. On the long walk back I decided we just had to go swimming. So when I got to the house I told them it was okay. During the swim I told them to swim very low on the water and keep their heads below the bank of the ditch. Something must have gone wrong because he found out about it and I got a spanking that night.

In 1927, Mom went in the hospital to have a baby in Idaho Falls, Idaho. I remember Sherman and I talking about wanting a girl for a sister and sure enough it was Marilyn. She was a welcome addition to our family, a beautiful young lady in every respect.

It was here where I first remember the threshers in the fall of the year. All the neighbors would come and help, and the farm that had the threshing going on would, of course, have to furnish meals for the threshers. The farm wives would always try and outdo each other preparing good food. I'll never forget how much they ate and some of the comments.

I earned some very small change by trapping mice and being repaid one cent a piece. Without refrigeration and with just cellars to keep things cool, we had to keep the cellars mice-free as well. I participated in onion eating contests and I often wonder why I ended up liking them at all. I was a champion raw onion eater. At the age of six I didn't mind keeping others away from me.

I started milking cows on a regular basis at age 6 or 7. I was so good that I could shoot a stream of milk from the cow's tit into the cat's mouth sitting clear across the stable. Those cats loved that warm milk and the way they would wash their face and lick their paws was a joy to me, especially in the winter time when it was cold outside.

My best early Christmas recollections occurred here and they are very clear. Receiving my very first toy wind-up train and a Pollyanna game from my aunt and uncle Perkins in California were among my many and most vivid recollections. The Perkins, in our view, were rich relatives because they lived in California and he was an engineer on a freight train. They always sent a big package of presents, which really made our Christmas because we didn't get too many bought goods on the meager income from the farm. The Perkins' package was the hit of the season.

I began riding horses about this time with my brother, sister, and cousins.

We grew wheat, potatoes, and green beans in abundance, but there was always something that kept us from making much more money than it cost to run the operation. Nevertheless, we had a good life with plenty to eat and lots of love.

The ground was very poor in this part of Idaho where this farm was located and Dad was trying to find a better place. In 1927 he located one about one mile east of Rigby next to the Burgess Canal. We hated to leave our friends, but it was only about 2 ½ miles so the move wasn't that bad. The house on the farm by the Burgess Canal was down a long lane, off the main road and tucked away; we thought it was a very neat location. It was a wonderful place for a growing boy.

Our Second Rigby Home (1927–34)

I particularly remember the tough winters and the snow so deep it covered the fence tops. We had three dogs that my brother, Sherman, had trained to pull sleds and people on skis. He would come out of the front door of the house and the dogs would about knock you down trying to get in the harnesses; they really loved to pull. We could get on skis behind them and head out across the fields all the way to town without having to worry about fences. We entered the dogs in the annual sled races in town and Sherm won most of the races for a single up to three-dog teams. He was great with animals and they all loved him.

As soon as it snowed, we could not take our car out because of that long lane and the deep snow, so we went to town with the horses and bobsled. It was quite a ride because the snowdrifts that came across the roads made high and low places. We went up and down these hills of snow and it was always a thrill.

In the daytime if Dad had to go anywhere in the bobsled, we tied a rope on the back and he pulled us on skis. That was our recreation. We would beg Dad at night to hook up the horses to the bobsled to go into town with our friends. The horses had new sharp metal shoes on and they wouldn't fall on the ice and snow. We started under a street light and he had the horses go very fast and then turn quickly and throw the sleigh around and it skidded around and around and around. The horses learned to pull against the sled so that it just kept flying. That was great sport. We went to school in the winter time in bobsleds with a school type cab on it that was covered to keep us warm. Those were very cold rides with no extra heat.

One of the biggest adventures, while we lived here, was the annual trip to the mountains with a team of horses and the running gear of a wagon to haul pine trees in for our winter wood. While in the mountains we would pick wild mountain huckleberries for Mom's special pies. Sherman and Dad would go after them the most, but on special occasions I could join them. On one trip, Dad let us take saddle horses to ride along the wagon and that was exciting. I remember one year when just Dad and I went. This was in 1932. Dad didn't have a watch and I had been given an old dollar pocket watch that was in bad repair, but I was very proud of it. I had managed to get it running and Dad would please me by often asking what time it was.

Sherm and I had wanted a sister, and we were thrilled when Marilyn was born in 1927

When I had to stay home from adventures, I was assigned a certain number of rows of sugar beets to hoe each day. By working fast, I could finish by 2:00 p.m. and go fishing or swimming in the big canal that bordered the farm. The canal was more like a river, and one fun thing we did was to tie a rope to the flume that took the irrigation water across to the hayfield on the north side of the river. On the end of this rope we would tie a few good sized boards nailed together and make a surfboard out of them. The water was running so fast that you could stand up and scoot back and forth across the river on the surf board. We used to charge two apples for other kids to use it.

I had to work very hard as a young man in the sugar beet fields. We had a very small, unproductive farm. The soil had a lot of rocks and we worked hard for what little we got back. I remember the trails in the winter through the snow to the piles of sugar beet tops. After we had cut the tops off, we put them in piles to feed to animals. The trails were cut through by rabbits from all over the countryside coming through the snow to get into our supply. On my tenth birthday, I had to work topping sugar beets so I couldn't have a party. In the middle of one of the rows and working very hard, I heard some young people coming singing happy birthday. It was Harold and Wayne Dowdle and the Chapman girls. They came to where I was working and brought me some presents, a pair of gloves—which I put to use immediately—and gum and candy. It turned out to be a ten-minute party on the 10th of October 1930, but I'll never forget how great it was to have them come by and recognize me. Little things like that meant a lot.

I was a little envious of kids who didn't have to work on a farm and I felt a little tied down, but I never did feel resentful. The family was so good to me and I felt I was important to our family's survival. I felt grown up and important and that I was helping to put food on the table for my family.

My good friend Harold Dowdle's father made my first pair of skis for fifty cents out of two boards. He steamed the ends and turned them up, and put a reinforcement piece on the front of each ski so that they wouldn't stick into the snow banks. We skied across the fence lines with a sail made from an old sheet, letting the strong wind push us a distance, and then made the long trek back. The fun was a good break from our hard work.

Sherman had some hay fever and I didn't, so I had a lot of hay to pile alone.

I hoped somebody would watch me and think, "look at that little boy out there going so fast and putting that hay in piles so quickly."

In elementary school, Sherm and I had to take a few weeks out of school in the fall to help with the harvest. I was always very good in math and science and the time away didn't seem to affect how I did there. However, my English scores suffered and I had to work hard to catch up.

We owned a Model T Ford, and one time Dad slaved away with it to get it running so he could take us on a trip. He worked on it almost all day because he wanted to take us to Idaho Falls to see the circus. I helped in every way I could and finally he got it finished and we did get down to Idaho Falls to see the circus.

The Cowboy Pilot Sparks my Passion for Flight

My first real captivation with flight and interest in airplanes was here in Rigby when I was about ten years old. Somewhere, I came across a book about an airplane pilot who ran out of gas and had to land in the desert. The pilot had died for lack of water and an old cowboy happened along and found the airplane sitting there in the sagebrush and found the pilot.

I was sorry for the pilot, but that old cowboy slowly taught himself to fly that airplane and found a way to get the gasoline for it. I was so excited that a cowboy could do something like that. It sounded like such an adventure, and I began to believe that maybe I could do that too.

My First Lesson in the Joy of Service

When I was about twelve years old, I was home alone one day on our farm in Rigby, Idaho and the folks had gone to visit and I didn't want to go. It got dark and I knew the cows had to be milked. There were seven of them and four of them were already at the barn. When the folks didn't come, I got the rest of the cows in. As I began to milk those cows, I started hoping that Dad wouldn't get home until I had finished and put the milk in the can. I knew he would be very surprised and pleased.

I milked faster and faster and I left the two mean cows till last, the ones that Dad had always had to milk. When I came to those cows, I tied them up and put the hobbles on the backs of their legs so they couldn't kick me and tied their tails down so they wouldn't hit me in the face with them. I worked at it very quickly and I was surprised to find that I could do it. All the time I was worried about when my family would return. As I poured that last bucket of milk in the big ten-gallon can, I saw the lights of our car coming down the long lane, and I made for the house.

Dad rushed in and announced the car had broken down on their return. I was so proud when Dad said, "Well son, let's go get the cows. I'll get the lantern and we'll get them milked."

I said, "Dad, those cows are all milked. I've got them all done." He asked, "You didn't get old Brindle milked did you?" And I said, "I got every one of them milked, Dad, every one, every last drop and the can is in the barn."

The look of disbelief on his face is one that I'll never forget. I felt so good about myself that I had done it without having to be asked. I found that real happiness comes from serving others in need as my parents had taught me and I had now experienced.

Noticing My Mother's Sacrifice

In 1933, when I was twelve years old and a Boy Scout, I became aware of my mother's sacrifice to send me to a big Boy Scout jamboree in Salt Lake City.

For several months, Mother had been putting small change away for a pair of new shoes from her earnings while working part time at a milliner's shop. The shoes were set aside at the local store until she could save enough money to pay cash. I remember her keen anticipation as her savings grew to almost three dollars. She reached the three-dollar goal the same week the scoutmaster rode by on his horse to tell the folks about the jamboree in Salt Lake. It was a jamboree on the big lawn just north of the Hotel Utah and a long way from our home in Rigby, Idaho in the big city—Salt Lake.

I had already told the scoutmaster and the troop I couldn't go. My time was completely taken helping Dad on the farm and there was just no money available for me to earn outside the farm work for special or regular jobs during those difficult times.

I was not bitter about working for my family on the farm. I had found the joy, even at a young age of "service before self." Because of who my parents were, I wanted to help all I could. However, Mom knew how much that scout trip meant to me and signaled Dad to reassure the scoutmaster that I could go. She knew about my adventuresome spirit and desire to know the world outside of Garland. After he left, I asked Dad where the money could come from and all he said was, "Don't worry."

The next day as I hurried off with the troop Mom pressed a small manila envelope into my hand. I will never forget that trip because when I got back home Mom still had on her old shoes, but a special light shone in her eyes. I am sure that light was there when I was born, and I saw it each time after that when she gave of her time and strength to do something special that made us happy. She looked the same way when we did things to make her proud of our actions. We warmly exchanged greetings and then I fully realized that my trip had taken the place of Mom's new shoes.

I had wondered where the three dollars for the trip had come from, but my selfishness kept me from admitting it must have come from my mother's shoe fund until that moment when I realized she was still in her old shoes (May 8, 1977 Mother's Day Bishop's Message by Gail Halvorsen, bishop).

These dogs were my constant companions on the Garland farm in 1939. The black dog chased aircraft rather than cars.

Chapter Two: Life in Utah

Jack Rich's Ranch (1934–36)

Jess Earl again had a major influence in the life of our family. He contacted Dad and asked him to come back to northern Utah and help him run a big ranch called Jack Rich's Ranch. It was a time when there was no money, but Jess Earl said that he would pay him a salary and also give him some grain to help us with food. I wanted to go very badly because our idea of life on Jack Rich's ranch was that it would be glamorous. Our dream came true as arrangements were made. Sherm and I had heard about the amount of livestock there, and that it was a ranch on the Oregon Trail with a big fresh-water spring on it. It was the Wild West where Native Americans had lived before the pioneers came through. It was complete with bucking chutes, arrowheads to find by the spring, rumors of a gambler shot in the house, and cowboy Ed living in the bunkhouse.

We moved onto the ranch in 1934 and it was a boy's dream. It was on the mountain straight west of Fielding, Utah. The house was again isolated up a long lane.

There were horses to ride and calves to put in the bucking chutes just like a rodeo. One of the biggest group of bucking horses in Utah was kept there in the summer time to fatten up and then to take on the rodeo trail. We used the bucking chutes for calf riding and had a lot of fun. Sherman came down from Rigby High School and joined us there. I couldn't wait to take him back in the mountains and show him the beautiful places, the glens, and the groves of trees. I also couldn't wait to take him to shoot wild chickens, prairie chickens, and

I enjoyed school and had excellent teachers who supported my interest in science and mechanical things.

grouse, for which there was no hunting season at that time.

It was a wonderful place for a boy and his dog and I had a wonderful dog. When Sherm was gone, and without other boys and girls to play with, I played with the dog. I would take him into a huge barn, make him stay, and then hide and whistle so that he came looking for me. When he finally discovered me, he would bark, jump up on me, and lick my face. We spent hours playing hide and seek.

By this time, I was in the eighth grade and wanted to ski very much. I had no money for new skis and the pair that Harold Dowdle's dad had made for me had long since broken and had come apart. Sherm and I found a barrel with long staves so we nailed leather straps in the middle and made barrel stave skis from them. We waxed them to make them very slick and then went up the mountain into a steep ravine. We had a wonderful time skiing straight down the edges of this steep ravine

In my eighth grade math class we were seated according to our standing in the class. I was always in the first row and several times in the first seat in the first row. My interest in science and things mechanical increased rapidly.

I learned to drive many horses, as many as eight heads of horses pulling a harrow working the fields, and dad working even more than that on the ploughs. He ploughed up the land to plant the wheat and then harvested it for food. We had a fair-sized garden, we raised animals for the meat, and kept our churned butter and vegetables in the root cellar. We always had something to eat there and never went hungry. We developed a feeling of gratitude for this because we knew that others were having a very tough time during those years.

A Heartbreaking Loss

One of my primary role models growing up was my brother, Sherman, who was five years older than me. It seemed like he could do everything—he had lots of physical strength, he had talent and ability, he was serious about his schoolwork, and he loved life. He was also, along with my father, my hunting and fishing companion.

Sherm also wanted to be a forest ranger, and I remember him studying without electricity by kerosene lanterns and, a little later, by the more modern Coleman gas lanterns, all the different shrubs and materials and scientific kinds of things that he was so interested in. He set an example for me on the importance of an education.

In addition to all his other talents, Sherm was a talented musician. He played the trumpet so well that he was in demand all over the valley to play in dance bands. We didn't have a car because the car we had bought in Rigby was without a license—Dad didn't have enough money to pay for license plates—but that didn't stop Sherm. He often got rides home from those who played with him in the bands. Other times he had to walk and wouldn't get home until two or two-thirty in the morning.

A terrible tragedy came for our family in the fall of 1934. Sherm and I had ridden in the cold November rain to bring in a number of cows that were on the range before winter set in. Sherm didn't want to quit and we stayed longer than we should have. Finally, he brought in the last ones by himself, chilled to the bone, and developed a bad cold.

After some weeks, his illness did not improve, and he was in bed with a raging fever. The local doctor came out and said they would have to get him to the hospital right away and we had better take him to Salt Lake City, which was eighty-five miles away, because he would need the best care. The doctor was afraid for Sherm's life.

The disease progressed more rapidly than we could have imagined possible and soon he was in an oxygen tent. Dad and Mom went to Salt Lake and stayed by his bedside and I stayed with Jess Earl in Fielding. Early one morning I heard the phone ring—it was a report that Sherman had passed away and they couldn't do anything to save him.

It was a heartbreaking loss. He was a great companion and teacher. We had our normal spats as brothers do, but I adored him and looked up to him.

Some thought it was pneumonia, but pneumonia was quite well known. The doctor thought it was a very severe case of polio. There were others who thought it might have been diphtheria, but I don't believe the cause of death was ever fully known. At that time there was no penicillin available and there was no medication that would reduce the raging fever that he had.

Sherm's death devastated my parents. My mother had planned that Sherm would be a missionary for our church. We were doing all that we could even though we had no money—hoping that there would be some way he could go on a mission. She could not understand why he would be taken when he was in the throes of making these preparations. At this time, Dad became concerned about our solitude at Jack Rich's ranch and started to look for another place closer to town where there would be neighbors.

After Sherman passed away, the ranch was not the same. While living on the property isolated from other young men and young women, I would often take long hikes or rides alone with my dog, my gun, and a horse back up in the mountains, climb to the highest point, and gaze out across the valley which seemed to intensify my love for the outdoors and the creation around me.

My brother's passing brought home to me the value of human life. At his death, I realized Sherm was the age of many young men who had lost their lives in war. Because of my parents' and my anguish at his loss, I developed a deep well of compassion for others' suffering.

My Father and the Bit of the Horse

My father had little schooling past high school, but the lessons he taught me about life were worth more than if he had a PhD. He had an innate ability to fix anything, work with wood, and make whatever we had to have. He worked with people extremely well. He loved to fish and hunt for family food, and work with horses. He had about six horses helping with his harrow, as we never ever had a tractor. Horses seemed to calm down for him. On Jack Rich's ranch, in the summer, they kept horses for rodeo for the fall, and after a summer on the range, he evaluated them and trained some for plowing. That was the most extreme case I remember ever about him and horses—using bucking horses to pull his harrows.

I credit my father with bringing to my attention at a very early age the importance of little decisions and how they affect you on the road of life. My first real lesson in this was probably in high school, when I was helping with the sugar beets. We had four horses to help pull the wagon and we had to throw the beets up into the wagon and then take them about two miles to the factory.

My father compared a bit in the mouth of old Ned, one of the lead horses, to how small things make a big difference. He brought me over to him and then he raised the lips of Ned to show me the bit in his mouth.

"See this bit?" he asked. "It is a small piece of metal. But it can turn the whole horse and influence the direction of what the horse can accomplish. Your small decisions will set you on your path of life!"

I think the reason I became the Candy Bomber was because of what my father said about little things. He taught me the importance of paying attention to and then following little but important feelings that come to us. The little things add up to set us on our life's path.

Sugar Beets, Sports, and Work on the Garland Farm (1936–41)

Dad wondered now, especially with Sherman gone, where we could go to be with more people because it was extremely lonely for Mom. Dad had a chance to take what little money he received from the place in Rigby, Idaho and buy a small farm just on the outskirts of Garland, Utah, in 1936. That was a come down for me from the ranch and the wild setting in which it was placed, but it was time for me and my younger

car trouble?

In Garland, I acquired an old 1924 Maxwell car, the first of many
I tinkered with, and learned how to fix it and keep it running

sister, Marilyn, to interact with others and move Mom closer to town.

The new farm was small, perhaps twenty acres. It was dedicated to sugar beets, which wasn't anything new to me after living in Rigby. We also had some alfalfa and grain. After a time, my father had a chance to add twenty more acres to the farm.

Besides raising sugar beets, the farm work included chores with the cows, horses, chickens and pigs. In the early morning, late at night, and even on

Saturday, I helped clean out the chicken coop if there was no farm work to do. We had a good-sized chicken coop with a lot of white leghorns that laid well. Dad took good care of them because that was the only cash crop that we had during the year except for when we harvested the sugar beets.

We had no indoor bathrooms until my father built one onto the back of the house, and we had to haul in water for a year before my father dug a trench to bring city water to our home. We did have electricity in the house and lights, which we did not previously have. It was during this time that I wanted to hunt, but it was different without Sherman. I didn't have a gun at that time, and I worked for Jess Earl putting up hay until I earned enough that he gave me a double-barrel shotgun. There were a lot of pheasants on the farm, and every pheasant season, my dog and I would get the limit, usually a few extra. The shotgun had hammers on the outside like the one that Daniel Boone would have had. When a pheasant would fly up I could hardly get it to my shoulder and it would kick me black and blue, but I'd get my share of pheasants.

Our next door neighbors were Dean and Dorothy Capener and their children, Bill, Dorothy, Mary, Caroline, and Pam. Bill was my closest friend during that time. He liked to hunt and fish and ride horses. We worked very hard, so the little time we got off was appreciated.

I acquired an old car, the first of many I tinkered with, and learned how to fix it and keep it running. We had a lot of great fun in that old car.

In the spring on the farm, I thinned the sugar beets. Later in the summer, I weeded them. It was best to not look at the whole field of ten acres at once because the job of thinning out those solid rows of sugar beet plants to a single skinny root every eight inches would become overwhelming. The hoe handle was twelve inches, which could be worked back and forth while bent over, sometimes moving along on my knees and keeping my nose close to the hoe. It stirred up the dust in my face. Thinning sugar beets was about the only job one could get cash for in farm work during the tough times of spring 1939. The job was a real taskmaster and professor of discipline for the ten hours a day, six days a week that it required.

My first deer hunt was in October of 1936. I was just sixteen, and it was the first year I could get a license. Dad was very busy, but he said, "I'll take you." He seldom could get away, so it was a real thrill for me. We still had the old car from Rigby. We went out to Park Valley to a place that Dad had heard about. We went up an old mining road to a deserted log cabin mine shack located on the south slope of the Raft River Mountains. We made our bed in the cabin and the next morning we got up at 4:00 a.m. and started to hike up the mountain. When we were halfway up, Dad said he would stop there where he could watch the surrounding canyons. I told him I wanted to go further. I didn't know at that time that Dad was bothered with a bad heart and it was all he could do to get to that point. That

In 1936, Dad moved our family to a small farm in Garland, where we would be closer to other people. I revisited our Garland home in 2016 with four of my children. It looks much newer now than it did when we moved in!

heart was to claim his life fourteen years later in a heart attack on the little farm they moved to later in Modesto, California. Well, I made it to the top of the mountain just as the sun rose, and under very exciting circumstances, I found myself in a herd of deer. I got a big buck and later on, a man came by on a horse. I paid him one dollar to take it off that mountain down to the old mining cabin. I was very proud, but sad that Dad didn't get one.

Of course I brought the long-legged American saddle horse I had trained for Sherm with me to Garland. Those

occasional times when I had a few hours would find me high on the west mountain with my dog, my gun, and my horse marveling again at the creation of nature and the panorama laid out below. Moving and working so much, it was hard for me to develop friends except for Bill next door. Old Shep, our black cattle dog and retriever, was my constant companion.

The sport I loved best was ice hockey, and in North Garland, we had a lot of good hockey players. We formed a team called the North Garland Eagles, and I was one of the best players. I still have a crooked nose to show for it. I enjoyed basketball, but played organized ball only in the church league. My highest pole vault with the old solid pole was eleven feet and two inches.

Our winter recreation consisted mainly of skiing behind saddle horses around town. People shoveled their driveways and under the street lights, which gave us a good ski jump. At night we traded off riding the horse and riding the skis. When we tired one horse, we'd go back to get another.

Lorraine Pace

Lorraine was the only girl I dated the spring of my senior year at Bear River. Some of those dates were in the old Maxwell car I had got running and fixed up. Lorraine was from a remote cattle ranch in Southern Utah and was staying with her aunt for a short time before returning to her family. When she showed me a photo of her in chaps, the reins of her saddle horse in one hand and the lead rope of a packhorse in the other, I knew I wanted to get to know her. However, at the end of the school year, she returned to southern Utah and eventually married. I graduated from high school and worked in addition to finishing a refrigeration course I had been taking. Soon I would begin pilot training. Pearl Harbor would happen, and our paths would not cross again until many years later. A few years later I met Alta, and we wrote for about six years until we were married. Sixty-three years later in 1999, after Alta's tragic death and the death of Lorraine's husband, Lorraine and I were married.

The B26 twin-engine light bomber became my favorite airplane to fly while in Natal. There were just two of them there and we could use them for recreational flying. We did not use them for regular runs; we flew transport airplanes. It was a pressure release to fly these "hot" airplanes that could do maneuvers. We often reenacted make-believe dog fights while flying them.

In Brazil, as well as in other places I served, an American in uniform was fair game on the street for kids with a sweet tooth. It became a conditioned response; a group of kids, their immediate, strong request, hand in the pocket for pre-placed goodies for such an encounter, and the pleasure of dispensing the same.

Chapter Three: Born to Fly

Looking Up

Our field in Garland lay almost directly beneath the airway from Salt Lake City to Malad, Idaho. Every once in a while, the sound of an aircraft would come over that quiet valley and provide an occasion to straighten up and look. I would watch those beautiful airplanes gracefully glide through the blue sky above and wonder how it would be to pilot such a machine far from the clods and dust.

The sight of a silver shaft against that beautiful blue western sky and the sound that kept it there sent a shiver down my spine each time the event was repeated.[1]

Later that summer I was hoeing weeds in the beet field when I suddenly became aware of the sharp staccato beat of an increasing roar coming in from the west. The source was an aircraft, not in the airway, but headed straight for me at tree top level. I had no thought to hide; in my ignorance I wanted to get as close as I could. At the last possible second the sleek bi-plane pulled up vertically. The prop wash cooled my face but my heart was in my throat and my feet were off the ground. Too soon it was a tiny speck and then gone. I knew then that I just *had* to learn to fly!

The following weekend, a neighbor friend of mine, Arthur Hansen, came home from Utah State University in Logan for a visit. It was he who had flown over the farm and given me that hair-raising demonstration.

"How did you like that, Seymour?" he queried with an expectant grin on his

---

1 Halvorsen, Gail S., *The Berlin Candy Bomber* (Cedar Fort: Springville, 2017), 11.

face. He used my embarrassing middle name to help rub it in. "Sure beats playing nursemaid to a sugar beet!"

"How do I get started?" I pleaded.

"All you have to do is go to college, qualify as a sophomore, and pass a test and they will enroll you in the beginners' part of the flight program."

My heart sank. *Two years?* It would be easy to complete two years of college if I could only afford it and my dad could do without me on the farm. There was no way in the world that I could go to college given these constraints. I was the only one that Dad had left to help on the farm, and if that wasn't enough, there just were not any resources available. If there had been other funds, Dad would have gladly shared them.

The avenue used by my friend to learn to fly just wasn't open to me. Undeterred, I began reading all the books on flight I could find. Something would somehow turn up—and eventually it did in the form of non-college scholarships.

In high school, although I was a good athlete, my nights were taken up on the farm. I never really regretted that because Dad was always so good about it, recognizing that I was giving up some

of the things that I would like to do to help with that which had to be done.

With the help of excellent teachers, I excelled at math and science and worked on a home-study course in refrigeration to qualify for repairing home appliances. I graduated from Bear River High School in 1939 with an excellent record, but I still was not headed for college. After graduation, I finished up the refrigeration course with a few months in Chicago and took a job with Gamble's Skogmo in Tremonton. It was a store like Western Auto, and it carried all supplies necessary for survival in a rural environment. I also repaired refrigerators and freezers on the side.[2]

Just a few months after my high school graduation, Hitler attacked Poland. Feelings against Germany were growing stronger in the community and in my circle of friends and family. I never guessed that one day after eight years of world war, I would help feed Berlin's survivors.

After high school graduation and as I began working other jobs, I worried about my parents on the farm without my continuous help. I was able to still work a little on the farm, but not to the degree I had previously. It helped that

2   Halvorsen, Gail S., *Personal History* (1985).

we were able to share labors such as haying with neighbors. Also, the sugar beet company, U&I, gave farmers a cash advance in the spring to hire laborers to thin the beets. In the fall the advance would come out of the cash the company paid the farmers for the harvest.[3]

My Flight Scholarship, Pilot License, and CAP Wings (1940–41)

Before the United States became involved in the war, there was a non-college pilot training program put in place around the country to try to get more pilots interested in flying and trained to be pilots. We knew we would get involved in the war with Germany sooner or later and we didn't have enough pilots to mount any kind of offensive against the Germans. So they started a program for kids who weren't in college at the time. The scholarships would make it possible for many of us to get our pilot's license without having two years of college first.

All over the nation there were night schools to teach aviation, aircraft design, aerodynamics, aviation rules, regulations, and everything that had to do with flying an airplane. A course was held at Bear River High School, where

I had graduated, and I signed up for the course without hesitation. We took flight lessons at Brigham City Airport with Johnny Weir as our instructor. At the end of the course, we had a written test. To get a pilot's license, we had to pass the written test and also a flight test, and then ten flight scholarships would be awarded.

My determination to get one of those scholarships was only occasionally dampened by the thoughts of the other 120 contestants for those ten slots. The sugar beet was a powerful motivator. I received the sixth scholarship. When the ten of us got our scholarships, all of us put in $50 and bought an airplane—a piper cub with a 50-horsepower engine. It wasn't much of an airplane, but for $500, we had an airplane and it was at Brigham City Airport where we traded off flying it when we wanted to. That was good, but I didn't have money to buy gasoline to fly very often.

There were a number of my friends who were going into the service to learn to fly and they would buy my gasoline if I would take them out and let them fly and show them how to do it so it would help them to get into the Aviation Cadet program. I obtained my pilot license in September 1941, and soon after, I earned my Civil Air Patrol Wings. Of course, I had to take Dad and Mom and Marilyn

3   Gail S. Halvorsen, Interview by Denise Halvorsen Williams, August 2017.

for a ride right away and show off a little bit with them.

I loved to fly up over the farm and do tricks to let Dad and Mom know it was me up there in that shiny airplane. I would wiggle the wing of the airplane and occasionally do spins, but Mom thought I was going to crash one of those times, and told me if I did spins anymore she would make me stop flying. From then on I only wiggled the wings and stopped dive-bombing the farm. I appreciated very much the encouragement I received from Dad and Mom in my major decision to fly, which was viewed then as a very dangerous occupation. Neither one of them really discouraged me from learning to fly.

I put my heart and soul into that airplane, the program, and the theory that made it fly. The loops and spins were especially exciting. I had unwittingly taken the first step on the way to Berlin.

Losing a Friend to War

A number of my buddies went to the ground school with me at Bear River High in 1941. One of my best friends in the neighboring town of Tremonton, Conrad Stephan, had also applied for a scholarship, but he didn't get one and was very disappointed.

Conrad wanted to fly so badly, and his dad was a successful businessman with Tremonton Machinery, so he had access to more money than I did. He said, "I'll buy all the gas you need if you will fly with me and teach me how to do it."

So Conrad bought my gas and I flew a lot of hours. I thought I knew all about

Johnny Weir (in baseball cap) was my first flight instructor. He gave me my first lessons at Brigham City Airport in a plane like this one. Johnny had great personal relations, was patient, understanding, yet aggressive enough to keep us learning every day. He sensed where each of us was and what we needed to get on our own fast. I can never forget him. Photo taken in August 1989.

flying—I'd earned my private pilot's license and I could show him everything they taught me to get my license. We did everything—spins and stalls and what you had to do to recover from unusual positions. Conrad was a natural—he caught on immediately. I even let him land it one time. He did a great job and he just loved flying.

When Hitler came on the scene and the war started, he enrolled in the Aviation Cadet program, graduated with high honors, and became a fighter pilot in the military. They sent him to England to escort the bombers attacking over Germany in his P-47 Thunderbolt.

I think it was 1944 when the Germans shot down my best friend and killed him. I was deeply affected by the loss of Conrad, who I had trained and who had so much to live for. I was very bitter against the Germans and the intensity of that feeling lasted quite a long time.

War and Military Pilot Training (1941–42)

By 1941, it looked like the war was going to start and a big construction project at Brigham City developed where they were going to build a hospital for the military. Because of the exceptional wages being paid at Brigham City

($80.00 a week), I quit Western Auto and went there to work as a carpenter's apprentice.

Sunday morning December 7, 1941 dawned a clear and cool day, but after church it was warm enough to wash my car. I had barely got started, listening to the radio when the music program was interrupted and the announcement was made that the Japanese were bombing Pearl Harbor.

Things moved quickly after that. I decided that I wanted to apply for the Aviation Cadet Program in the United States Army Air Corps. I read in the newspaper where they would be giving tests in Logan, Utah. I took them on May 17, 1942 and passed them very well, was sworn in, and was offered an opportunity to go into the Air Force as a pilot trainee.

Because of the big pilot backlog, they suggested I go to school at Utah State for two quarters and then I would be called into active duty. By working at the hospital with the increased rate of pay, I paid off all of my debts and had enough money saved to go to Utah State in the fall of 1942. I was thrilled. This was my chance! I had wanted to go to college, but until now, I hadn't been able to afford to go.

I was worried about my parents working on the farm without my help. However, they were also making plans for their future that would free them from the backbreaking labor in Garland.

In the summer of 1942, just a few months before I left for Utah State, my mother's favorite sister, Jennie Perkins, and her husband, Dee, came to visit us from their home in Stockton, California. Over the years they had sent us Christmas packages and had occasionally come to visit.

After a few days with us, they, noticing our hard work and routine and also knowing I would be going to Utah State and then on to military service as a pilot, suggested that my parents and sister consider coming to Stockton to work in the Navy shipyards for the war effort. My father would work just eight hours a day, and the pay would be greater than the farm income.

My parents decided to lease the Garland farm, and in the fall of 1942, they moved to Stockton, where my father worked for three years at the Pollock Shipbuilding Company and then the Stockton Naval Supply Annex.[4]

---

4   *Luella Halvorsen Papers*, in possession of Denise Williams.

Utah State and Alta Jolley (1942–43)

I was at Utah State University for two quarters and I enjoyed the college environment so much. I hadn't realized what I was missing. I thoroughly enjoyed just learning and trying to discover new truths, which surprised me some. When I had first enrolled, they asked me what my major was and I had written down civil engineering. When I checked with the civil engineering department, they asked me to write down why I had selected engineering and I'll never forget the cocky, off-handed answer I gave: "I've got what it takes and it's got what I want."

The most important thing that happened to me at Utah State was when a beautiful, young lady asked me to a women's preference activity. I believe it was a sleigh ride and the snow didn't show up. My date, Alta Jolley, and I ended up just having a good time fooling around in the gym, climbing a rope, and swinging off the railing on the rope and then buzzing around town in my car.

Alta was raised in Zion National Park in one of the stone ranger homes just up the canyon from the park museum. Her father was Chief Ranger there from 1928–1943. Alta's mother and grandfather were also born where Zion

I went through basic military training with several friends at Shephard Air Force Base in Texas.

National Park is today. She was quiet, gracious, supportive, and hardworking. She loved the outdoors and adventure. Her outstanding quality was the way she lived the principle, "service before self."

I think Alta liked my car, so she did accept the next time I asked her out. I really thought that she was beyond my reach because she was one of the most popular young women at the university. Alta and I dated often, but I was also dating other girls and the time was going all too fast. I knew I would receive my active duty assignment in the Army Air Corps soon.

Assigned to Active Duty, Earning my RAF, and Army Air Corps Wings (1943–46)

One day in March 1943, while at Utah State, a note came to me to see the advisor for the Army Reserve. He handed me a long envelope. It was my orders to report for active duty. I was to leave Utah State on the 20th of March 1943. The letter reminded me that my folks were concerned about me flying in the military, but supported me in my enthusiasm to get started. The last night in Logan was spent on a date with Alta. I didn't realize it then, but I was departing on a military career that was to last until September 30, 1974.

Many of my friends went with me on the train from Salt Lake City. There was a great spirit in America at that time. Everyone was pulling together. People

I volunteered to do my military pilot training with the Royal Air Force who came to the U.S. to train. It was a wonderful experience to get to know other nationalities as well as I did.

By the time we went into the AT6 or the Harvard trainer, I was well on my way to mastering all the aerobatics required.

were singing songs on the train, being friendly to one another, and everybody was pulling for the country. It was a feeling I shall never forget.

My friends and I arrived in our civilian clothes in Wichita Falls, Texas, and went to Shepard Air Force Base. As we marched in in our civilian clothes, I can remember it yet. All the other people—recruits and military people in the barracks—lined the roadway as we carried our bags full of newly issued military clothes. They would yell at us from every barracks, "You'll be sorry, you'll be sorry." I remember the corporal who was in charge of our unit, who shouted back, "No they won't be sorry these are Aviation Cadets." I took a special pride from that moment on in

being a flyer. It just seemed to spur me on to do the very best I could.

From Shepard Air Force Base for basic training, we went to Stillwater, Oklahoma. At Oklahoma A&M University we had college instruction in sciences, meteorology, and math to help us in the flying program. We also had about ten hours of flying there to see if we were adept at flying and would make good pilots or not. Because of my past training, most of my time was training in aerobatics with my instructor and he told me right away that I had all I needed to be an excellent pilot.

We lived in some new, tar-paper shacks, and it wasn't the nicest living accommodations, but having a university atmosphere again was to my liking. A few months later when we were ready to ship out, I got a really bad case of the flu and they held me back one month until I got better. This caused a lot of my friends to go on ahead of me and left me a little bit alone. There was only one or two left who came from Utah—Dale Homer was one—and we went together to Lackland Air Force Base in San Antonio, Texas. Our cadet pre-flight training was there and it was very demanding, but they called us "gentlemen," and again I was very proud to be in the flying side of the business.

When I went into flight training in San Antonio, officers came to our class and said, "We need some volunteers to go into the Royal Air Force (RAF) for pilot training."

The RAF trained their pilots in the United States at that time because the Battle of Britain was going on and all the British airfields were crowded with fighters and bombers. They wanted some Americans mixed with them as a matter of international cooperation and public relations and to try their method of training. I volunteered and several

I received my Royal Air Force Wings from Wing Commander Roxborough on June 11, 1944. A few days later, an American instructor took us up to test us for our wings with the U.S. Army Air Corps. We had twice the amount of aerobatics as the Army Air Corps training, so we blew the instructor away.

friends
came with me.[5]

The Spartan School of Aeronautics in Miami, Oklahoma had a contract with the Royal Air Force. There were about five Americans to every twenty-five British airmen. We had a lot of gunnery training and fighter training. Because of my considerable flying experience, I spent a lot of time in advanced work.

---

5   Halvorsen, Gail S., *Personal History* (1985), 26.

By the time we went into the AT6 or the Harvard trainer, I was well on my way to mastering all the aerobatics required. I was designated as a Senior Cadet right after my primary training and that meant I was placed in charge of all the cadets in the British and American senior program. It was a wonderful experience to get to know another nationality so well as we did. There were cadets fromScotland, England, and other parts of the British Empire.[6]

It was a wonderful day when we pinned on our bars and our wings on June 16, 1944. Of course, the wings were Royal Air Force wings. A few days after receiving my RAF wings, a US Army Air Corp instructor took us up to test us for our wings with the US Army

---

6   Halvorsen, Gail S., *Personal History* (1985), 27.

In my first year flying in the South Atlantic Theatre, I flew passenger and cargo routes in a C-47, a two-engine airplane often called a "Gooney Bird." After that first year, I flew larger airplanes such as the C-54, which I would later fly in the Berlin Airlift.

Air Corp. We had twice the amount of aerobatics as the Army Air Corp training, so we blew the instructors away.

With the completion of my RAF and Army Air Corps training, I was all set to be assigned with the Army Air Corps. At that point of the war, there was a need for airlift pilots, and I was sent to Romulus Air Force Base in Detroit, Michigan as part of the Ferry Command. Our job was to take airplanes wherever they were needed and we flew just about everything from B17s to B24s, and C47s. Even though I was prepared to be a fighter pilot, I was sent to cargo and passenger hauling operations.

Brazil and the South Atlantic Theatre (1944–46)

I should say that initially, five of us had orders to go to India and fly over the Himalayan Mountains or "the Hump" into China. However, as we were on our way and before we got to Natal, Brazil, one of the B-25 Mitchell bombers that were used for pilot training crashed and killed about four of the pilots. All four were transport pilots, so they took us off the airplane at Natal with a message to hold us—five young, brand-new second lieutenants—to fly foreign air transport operations in Natal.

One of my good friends, John Wessale, from Cedar Rapids, Iowa, went to Natal with me, along with several others that were from the same pilot training school. We were flying C-47 "Goonie Bird" passenger and cargo routes in the South Atlantic Theatre and other airplanes as well. I was introduced to and checked out by Captain John Hudson as an aircraft commander in that wonderful aircraft, the Douglas C-54 Skymaster.

I enjoyed Natal very much. The climate was temperate; it wasn't too awfully hot, it cooled off at nights, and there was a great amount of flying to do. We were averaging about 125 flying hours a month. It was principally a passenger operation, and some cargo. The senior pilots were ex-airplane pilots that were brought in during the war to fly. They were super instructors.

Because it was a passenger operation, we had to fly 650 hours co-pilot before they would check us out as the first pilot. We chafed at that, so whenever we could, we flew one of the other airplanes that we could fly on our own. One was the A24, the scout bomber, a dive-bomber made by Douglas. It was a single-engine fighter plane and we had three of them, flying most of the time.

John Wessale, myself, and our other friends—including Bob Heath, who was another of my very best buddies in the Air Force and who had gone through Miami, Oklahoma with us—flew those three airplanes in formation. We flew into Brazil and buzzed the countryside, gliding along looking at the natives and having a wonderful time. This helped to get rid of our frustration at not being first pilots in the passenger runs. Passenger runs were up and down South America, back to Miami, Florida, to Ascension Island in the mid-Atlantic, and to Africa and England.

On our way overseas, we stopped in Miami, Florida, while we were processed for foreign travel. We stayed in the Floridian Hotel. It was a wonderful place and for a young farm kid, it was pretty much uptown. I got to know Miami and learned to like lobster and shrimp, if that took any learning. While there, every morning when we had roll call, the officers would ask who wanted to go deep sea fishing. Of course I was a nut and got there early every day to go out deep-sea fishing.

Down in Natal, we lived in tents for a little while, but not too long. We flew into Rio de Janeiro, which quickly became my favorite city. One of my high

My crew and I flew a C-54 named the Trade Wind an average of three times a week to Ascension Island out in the middle of the South Atlantic

Our flight schedule was strenuous. We would leave Natal at 10.00 pm and fly all night to take advantage of the stars and find our way to Ascension Island.

caught fire just as I started to enter the clouds beyond Sugarloaf Mountain. The flames began to flow all over the engine and all over the wing.

I quickly shut off the gasoline, feathering the engine. Then I came back and landed on one engine on that very short strip. It was the best landing I had ever made. Smoke was still coming out of the wing; but it didn't explode, for which I have always been grateful.

I also flew many trips into Ascension Island, which was a stop on the way to Africa and England. Those trips were not passenger runs. We were taking fighter bombers and other kinds of airplanes for the war effort. I spent many hours on Ascension Island, and there were submarines that operated in those waters and off the coast of South America to some degree. Many were putting up false signals around Ascension Island to try and lead aircraft off course and run them out of gas to crash in the ocean. Some did, but most, with the benefit of navigators who used sun lines and the stars, could navigate without the electronic guides.

Refusing a Command

After some time in Natal, we got two four-engine DC4–C54 airplanes, which

school teachers, Mrs. Jorgensen, had traveled to Rio before and had talked to us about this beauty.

On my first trip to Rio as first pilot (which meant I had the responsibility of the crew and everything else), as we were departing from Santos Dumont—a very short strip three-thousand feet long in the middle of the bay, dropping off in the water on both ends—my left engine

I wanted to fly very badly. I applied to be one of the pilots of those two airplanes, but the United States had sent down the crews for those airplanes and so we didn't even get a chance to fly them.

However, one of the crews got drunk while in Miami and got into a good bit of trouble. When they came back down to Natal, our Commander removed them from the airplane, told them they were through, and sent them back to the United States. This same commander had ordered me to drink with him at a welcome party they had when our five pilots first came to Natal, but I refused.

Although we had all applied to be a pilot of one of those airplanes, I was one of the two selected to be the first pilot. The reason, the commander said, was not because I was the best pilot or because I had as many hours as anybody else, but because I had refused to drink on his command. He said the order he gave me was an important thing for him now because he had somebody he could trust flying that airplane. His job was on the line if something happened to the airplane after sending the experienced crew home. The other crew that was experienced checked us out and one of the airplanes was assigned to me personally.

I flew a C-54 named the Trade Wind an average of three times a week to Ascension Island out in the middle of the South Atlantic. We delivered food, supplies, and personnel to the island, which served as a way station to Great Britain and Africa for war planes.

We would leave the mainland of Natal at 10:00 p.m. and fly all night to take advantage of the stars to find our way to that five-by-seven piece of rock. We would come into Ascension Island at sun up, and I always had them hold the fishing boat that went out each day to catch fresh fish for the garrison on the island. After landing, I went out with them to fish and we caught small tuna on hand lines. I enjoyed that very much.

On one trip in taking a B25 to Ascension Island, our navigator misjudged the time and he had us let down an hour early. We flew for an hour at low altitude and just before we ran out of gas we were able to spot the island up ahead and land. We were sure we were going to have to ditch in the ocean that time.

Fortaleza and the Amazon

From Natal our squadron moved to Fortaleza, Brazil, and had many missions to Belém and Amapá on the Amazon. A lot of our time was spent searching for pilots who had been forced down or crashed in the jungles of the Amazon River Basin. At that time, I used to fly the Catalina flying boat. It would stay up for twelve hours in search patterns over rugged country that had never been charted. Many times when we were down over the tree tops, we would see a wisp of smoke and find it to be a very primitive, native village whose people would run out with loincloths on and spears and bows and arrows in their hands. Once we even saw them shooting arrows at us from the ground. We also scared beautiful parrots and all different colored birds out of the huge mahogany trees that sprang from the floor of this great rain forest.

We often ended up in British Guiana searching for those who crashed. The canopy of the jungle was so thick it was almost impossible to see anything. We never located anybody. They would go under the canopy and disappear, never to be seen again.

I was in Belém on the Amazon one day and the operations officer had just received a part of some airplane equipment. The part was brought in by a native. It was a piece of a B26 that had crashed between Amapá and Belém right by a little mountain. We circled the mountain looking for a very long time. It was an interesting time searching, flying up and down that great Amazon River with wildlife everywhere.

Why I Stayed in the Military after the War

In 1946, the war was over and everybody was going home. I had enough years of service during the war to leave, but I had to stay back in Brazil and help fly people and equipment home to the United States from South America.

During that time, a regular army team came around and asked for those who wanted to stay in the Air Force to take a Regular Army test to see if they could qualify. I didn't want to stay, but I happened to be in Natal and there was nothing going on and I took the test just out of a lark. My friend Bob Heath was with me and he wanted to stay in the Air Force in the worst way. But he didn't get accepted and I did—the only one in Natal offered a regular Army Air Force commission to fly. I didn't accept it at first, but then they told me that if I were a regular officer they would send me to school and pay my way and all my books. To a farm kid, that sounded crazy, but they guaranteed me that would be the case; so I accepted.

That's how I happened to stay in the Air Force to make it a career. I felt I was too old at that time, about twenty-six, that I wouldn't have time to go through a normal university experience and get married and do all of the things that I wanted to do. This offered me a chance to keep flying, have my tuition and books paid, and draw my full salary while going to school.

I had a wonderful time there in Brazil, and I had many experiences flying in all kinds of weather conditions, unusual locations, and using all the knowledge of flight and training possible.

From South America I was sent to West Palm Beach, Florida to fly DC 4s and C54s, which I had experience flying to South America, Panama, Bermuda, and other foreign points. I was selected for Air Tactical School in Panama City, Florida. I also had a lot of vacation coming from being overseas, and spent some time driving and also flying out to visit my folks and Alta.[7]

---

7   Halvorsen, Gail S., *Personal History* (1985), 35.

Landing at Tempelhof was tricky. The runway was unpaved and a little short, which, for the Airlift planes and their heavy loads, didn't offer much room for error. In addition, bad weather frequently threatened to blow us off course.

The major cargo on the airlift was flour and coal. Flour arrived at Wiesbaden by rail and was then transferred to the cargo holds of C-47 and C-54 aircraft, which flew the supplies into Berlin. The aircraft tail is a B-17 assigned to the commanding general of the USAF in Europe, which was General Curtis LeMay first and later General John Cannon.

The most appreciated cargo by the children of Berlin—fresh, whole milk.

General William H. Turner assumed command of the Airlift on July 29, 1948. A few months later on October 14, he became commander of the entire Combined Airlift Task Force.

Tempelhof Airport

I was in this lineup of C-54's on the ramp at Tempelhof waiting to be unloaded. Later on, better scheduling and unloading efficiency set in place by General Tunner cut down on the number of aircraft waiting.

Flour for Freedom. Former combatants worked
around the clock in harmony for the right to choose.

One day after my daily flights in July 1948, I hitched a ride back to
West Berlin to take some pictures of the city and the airplanes. I noticed
and filmed women and elderly men rushing out to the landing strip in
between aircraft landings to oil and tar the cracks in the airfield, to
dump dirt and sand into holes, and make other repairs to the runway so it
could withstand the tremendous strain of aircraft landing every few minutes.

As Airlift pilots, we flew three trips a day, making it possible for an aircraft to land every few minutes day and night in Berlin. Our airplanes were unloaded by Germans and then distributed to the city. The gratitude I saw in the eyes of our former enemies touched my heart.

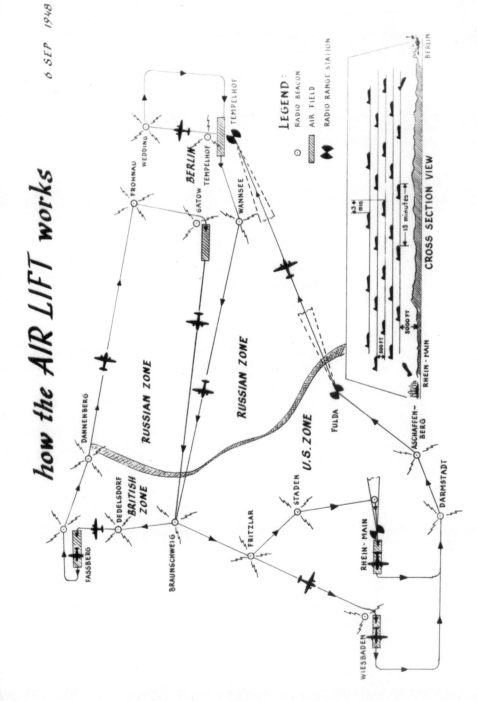

how the AIR LIFT works

6 SEP 1948

This diagram shows five flight altitudes which were later changed to two altitudes when better navigation and control equipment became available

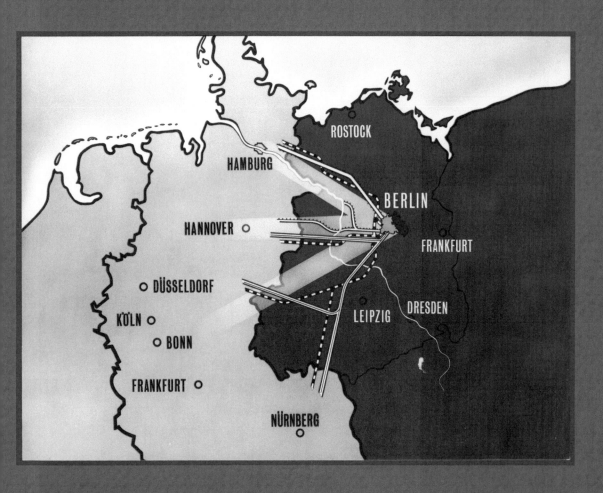

When the Soviets closed the land routes to West Berlin, cutting off more than two million people from the necessities of life, it became necessary to send supplies through three air corridors. This illustration shows which territory was controlled by the Soviets (dark gray) and which was controlled by the British, French, and U.S. (light gray)

PART 2

BECOMING THE
CANDY BOMBER

The crews on C-54 548 at Lajes Field in the Azores, en route to join the Airlift on July 11, 1948. Pictured from left to right are Capt. John H. Pickering, Lt. James L. Hunt Jr., Capt. Lawrence "Larry" Caskey, Lt. Everett E. Peyton, me, Lt. Guy B. Dunn Jr., and Capt. John M. Kelly.

The ramp at Rhein-Mein Air Base, which the majority of the C-54s flew out of early in the Airlift. The trucks belong to the Army 67th Transportation Truck Company.

RHEIN-MAIN AIR BASE - View from the control tower showing the arrival of military and civil supplies from Giessen Quarter-master Depot in trucks of the 67th Transportation Truck Company for transfer to waiting aircraft.

Chapter Four: The Berlin Airlift

Volunteering for the Airlift

In 1947, I was flying foreign transport out of Brookley Air Force Base in Mobile, Alabama. The military air transport service foreign operations primarily used C-54 and C-74 aircraft. I had checked out in the C-54 in Brazil and I wanted to take the next challenge of flying the huge C-74.

It was a monster airplane, the biggest one in the Air Force inventory, and a forerunner of the C124. There were only thirteen of them that were purchased and we had all of them. An opportunity came quickly, and I was transferred to the C-74 squadron. We were at Mobile just a short time before the Berlin Blockade occurred.

One day in July 1948, I was delayed flying the C-74 due to maintenance, and I noticed there was a C-54 squadron meeting, so I thought I would attend to see what was going on in that squadron. I found out they were going to announce which pilots would be called up to fly C-54s to Berlin to supply the citizens there with food and fuel. This operation would be called *Operation Vittles*. The enterprise was necessary because the Soviets had

The Douglas C-54 Skymasters, shown here on the ramp at Tempelhof Airport in Berlin, slowly replaced the C-47s in Airlift operations.

The American pilots most often used the southern air corridor. The French and British flew in from the north. All three allies flew out of Berlin using the center corridor. As an American C-54 pilot, I flew constantly from the Rhein-Main Air Base in Frankfurt and also Wiesbaden to Tempelhof Airport in West Berlin.

blockaded West Berlin, cutting off more than two million people in Berlin from the necessities of life. Most of them were women and children who had nothing to do with the German armed forces. That really got to me.

When the names were announced, I was not on the list to go because I was in the C-74 squadron, but one of my best friends, Pete Sowa, was called to go. He was married, and his wife had just given birth to twins when these orders came out for him to leave and fly the airlift in Germany in two days' time.

Pete wasn't there at the meeting because he was flying transport from South America and therefore had no knowledge of his new assignment. At the end of the meeting I went up and told the commanding officer that I was willing to take Pete's place, thinking he would not want to leave his family for six months. I also called his wife and talked to her about it, and she was happy I would volunteer to take his place.

I was adventurous and had no wife or children to worry about leaving behind. The squadron officers said I could make the switch back to the C-54 squadron to fly the Berlin Airlift, so it was a fluke that I went at all because I was not on the orders to go. The events that would lead me to a momentous meeting with the children at the end of the Berlin runway had been set in motion.

A Change of Heart

At the time of the Berlin Airlift, I was simply a cargo pilot who could fly day or night in any weather, carrying loads of all kinds to any place I was assigned. I did not know the politics going on at the time and the serious situation of the two-and-a-half million residents of Berlin who had been blocked by the Soviets from receiving food and goods.

A total of approximately 100 C-47 "Gooney birds" and more than 200 C-54s were used at the beginning of the Airlift. The C-47's were phased out after a few months. It was the most massive use of airpower for humanitarian reasons that the world had ever known.

The "Candy Bomber" on my first flight to Berlin.

I did know that people were hungry, were being used as political puppets, and that they needed our help. Those were enough reasons for me to want to do all I could to help.

My crew and I arrived in Germany on the 11th of July 1948, adding our C-54 to the mixture of C-47s and C-54s that were scattered about in front of the old brick control tower. The place was swarming with people and machines of all descriptions. Semi-trailer trucks loaded, unloaded, and in the process were everywhere.

We passed by a C-54 that was being loaded with sacks of flour for Berlin. I noticed down below the cargo door, on the ground, mixed with dirt and gravel was a small accumulation of flour over which was hovering a raggedly dressed man with a little sack and what appeared to be a small clothes brush. Even in the time it took us to pass he had the little treasure in the bag and with a furtive glance was back to work loading the aircraft. *If that flour is so valuable here, what in the world must it be like in Berlin?* I thought as we hurried on.

The dynamics of the moment temporarily overcame my fatigue and I began to marvel at the dedication and intensity of the members of the American military who, not long ago, had been bent on exterminating the

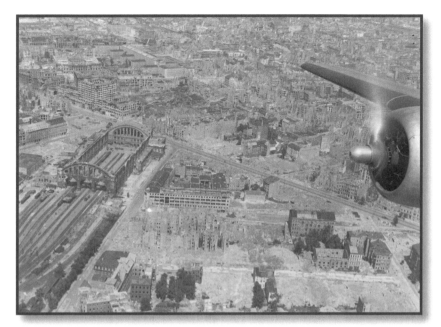

My C-54 wing over one of the main aiming points for British and American bombers, the Anhalter Bahnhof, a crucial target in the center of Berlin The subway tunnels under the Bahnhof became tombs for hundreds when the tunnels were flooded during the last battle.

Germans and were now dedicating their all to saving the Berliners.

I reflected on my own feelings about the German people. There was much in the media about the hardness of the Germans, the atrocities, and the claims of superiority. Some Americans had offered a defense by blaming the reported behavior on Hitler and his policies and not on the nature of people.

Some of the airlift pilots had bombed Germany and Berlin during the war and we had all felt that the Germans were the enemy. Our folks at home who were not involved as soldiers or pilots, had very negative feelings toward the Germans too. I thought of Conrad Stephan who had been shot down and killed. Now, the pilots who had once bombed Berlin wanted to do all they could to help feed them! I found this to be absolutely remarkable.

On my first trip to Berlin, I did not know what to expect to see when I would meet Germans. Would there be a cold gaze—a superior or defiant look? How would I feel about these people who had formerly been the enemy and caused so much human suffering around the world?

The hum of the engines of Airlift airplanes was the heartbeat for parents and children alike in Berlin. Airlift logistics became a game for the kids to pass the long seige hours. Their bricks are in the shape of the Tempelhof hanger

However, these last feelings of doubt left me when I landed that first load of 20,000 pounds of flour at Tempelhof Airport in West Berlin. The German unloading crew poured through the open cargo door in the back of my aircraft when we landed. The lead man came toward the cockpit with moist eyes and a hand thrust out in friendship. His words of gratitude were unintelligible, but his expression and body language said it all. He looked at the bags of flour and back to us like we were angels from heaven.

People were hungry for food and freedom. We were giving them both and they were most grateful. Gratitude is the magic potion that makes enemies friends and seemingly impossible tasks doable. From then on, the pangs of doubt were gone. The tension was gone. How could this be? Almost instantly, we were brothers working for a common cause.

One of my fellow Airlift pilots had bombed Berlin during the war. I asked him how he felt about flying day and night on behalf of the enemy—the very ones who did their best to kill him as he flew over Berlin in 1944. He hesitated a moment, shuffled his feet and then said, "It feels a lot better to feed them than it does to kill them."

Another pilot added, "I didn't feel good about dropping the bombs. Now maybe I can do something about the food. I'm ready to go."

I only knew of one person who complained of flying day and night in behalf of a former enemy. This, I believe, was because of the overt expression of gratitude by the West Berliners. Everyone feels peace in their heart when they serve others. This was the case even though the "others" were the former enemy.

By the end of the airlift, thirty-one American and thirty-nine British pilots had given their lives to feed their former enemies. They were the true heroes of the Berlin Airlift.

A Sightseeing Trip to Berlin and Meeting the Children

The Allies had access to three air corridors into West Berlin and I was assigned to the American access at Rhein-Main in West Germany. As Airlift pilots, we flew three trips a day, making it possible for an aircraft to land

As I stood taking pictures, my eye caught on a group of about thirty kids in the middle of a grassy strip watching the planes. During my conversation with them, I was impressed by the value they placed on their freedom and their self-control in not asking me for candy as others had done.

I took this picture of Brandenburg Gate. To me, it was the epitome of the transformation of Germany from the glory of the early days to the destruction and desolation of the post-war era

Berlin sites, I had to schedule a military jeep and driver.

I noticed and filmed women and elderly men rushing out to the landing strip in between aircraft landings to oil and tar the cracks in the airfield, to dump dirt and sand into holes, and make other repairs to the runway so it could withstand the tremendous strain of aircraft landing every few minutes. Women made use of their waiting time by knitting needed socks, hats, sweaters, and mittens for loved ones or to barter. I marveled at their often cheerful attitudes as they worked to keep the airstrip repaired.

every few minutes day and night in Berlin. Our airplanes were unloaded by Germans, and then we flew right back to Rhein- Main.

One day, instead of sleeping after I had finished my flights, I hitched a ride back to West Berlin on one of our C-54s on an Airlift mission. I thought the airlift wouldn't last long, and I wanted to see a little of Berlin and take some pictures of the airlift airplanes landing since we had no time to do that while making our flights. While there, I received permission to take videos of the planes flying overhead. To get to the end of the runway at Tempelhof and see some

At the end of the runway at Tempelhof, after filming several airplanes popping up over the apartment buildings for the difficult landing, the first thing that caught my eye was about thirty kids in the middle of a grassy strip watching the planes swoop over the rooftops and land just behind where I was standing. Behind a barbed wire fence, now the children were watching me, an American pilot in uniform. By the time my Revere movie camera had recorded a few feet of film with aircraft seemingly popping out of the chimneys, half of the kids were right up against the fence across from me.

It didn't take long to exhaust my German vocabulary with, "Guten Tag, wie gehts?" I was immediately greeted with a torrent of responses that were geared to someone with a greater command of the language. We were soon joined by the rest of the children.

It was a mixed group. Most of them were between the ages of eight and fourteen, with an even split between boys and girls. They were not especially well dressed, but their clothes had been kept clean and in good repair. After an animated discussion between themselves, they appointed two or three as spokespersons for the group. Children were taught English in the schools and several of the kids spoke it quite well.

The children were very interested in the airlift operations dedicated to their survival. Some children were timing aircraft arrivals and could tell of the weekly increases in the number of landings.

One of the first questions was, "How many sacks of flour does each of the aircraft carry?" There had been some discussion about how many equivalent loaves of bread came across the fence with each airlift. Were we really flying in fresh milk for the younger children? What about the other cargo? How many tons? One question came right after the other.

Then I received a lesson about priorities. They were interested in freedom more than flour. They fully recognized that there was a real relationship between the two, but they had already decided which was preeminent. I was astonished by the maturity and clarity they exhibited in advising me of what their values were and what was of greatest importance to them in these circumstances.

In the months since the aircraft over Berlin changed their cargo from bombs to flour, the children had witnessed an accelerated change in international relations. These young kids began giving me the most meaningful lesson in freedom I ever had. Here I was, an American, almost bald-headed at the age of twenty-seven, and yet I was learning about something I obviously took too much for granted.

One of the principal spokespersons was a little girl of about twelve years with wistful blue eyes. She told me, "Almost every one of us here experienced the final battle for Berlin. After your bombers had killed some of our parents, brothers, and sisters, we thought nothing could be worse. But then we saw firsthand the communist system. We've learned so much more since that time. We don't need lectures on freedom. We can walk on both sides of the border [there wasn't a Wall then]. What you see speaks more strongly than words you hear or read."

Another boy continued, "We have aunts, uncles, and cousins who live in East Berlin and in East Germany and they tell us how things are going for them. When they are here they use our library to read what is really going on in the world. They can say what they think when they are over here."

Those who had parents, or a single parent, or only brothers or sisters, all believed that someday there would be enough to eat, but if they lost their freedom they feared they would never get it back. The wistful blue-eyed girl made the point that they could get by with very little for quite a while as long as they knew they could depend on us to stick by them and do the best they could.

Clearly it was freedom, not flour, that those children were concerned with on that warm July afternoon in 1948.

The conversation labored as it had to be given the language barrier, coupled with its interest, consumed much more time than I had allowed. My thoughts returned to the jeep and the driver and my worry was that he would not wait. More than an hour had already passed. The girl said more, but her words were washed away by four Twin Wasp R-2000 engines directly over our heads, responding to a pilot's demand for a little cushion to break his descent before impact with the runway. The added power was enough, but even then you could see the main landing gear struts almost bottom out.

In a moment, I whirled to go to the jeep, then paused long enough to thank the children for our talk, to reassure them that more planes and crew members were coming every day, and to marvel to myself about what I had heard and learned from those so young.

So these were the enemy? Or was the enemy just their leaders or the system? Were any of these Hitler's youth? Somebody was. What did they really think of the situation now? Were they being honest with me or telling me what I wanted to hear?

But my preconceived prejudice was melting like the proverbial January thaw. The children got to me more than the flour-unloading crew had. My heart had changed and my prejudice had completely washed away.

Little Decisions and Two Sticks of Gum

Often it is small and simple events that change the course of our lives. We cannot possibly know ahead of time what these are. We can only look back to be grateful we followed an intuition or made a wise choice at that critical moment.

As I walked away from the children at the fence after our long conversation, I called, "Sorry kids, I must go," and waved over my shoulder. My overriding thoughts were to get to that jeep and make up for precious lost time. It would be nice to get back to Rhein-Main in time to have one or two hours sleep before our flight shifts started again. In that frame of mind it was unlikely that a totally different, outside thought could get inside my head and affect my course of action, but it did.

At first it was hard to identify the intruder, this new thought. It was ever so soft, so small a probe as to be indistinguishable. But there it was. By now I was fifty yards away, headed for the jeep, but my mind was still back at the fence.

What made those kids so different? Again the probe got in with a little more persistence. It was quickly answered: *They are mature beyond their years. They have been through experiences and come to conclusions that are not representative of children at this point in their developmental cycle.*

But why are they different, in what other way?

I stopped in my tracks. *They had forgiven a former enemy in uniform.* But that wasn't all . . . The answer came with a rush. *Not one of almost thirty kids, most of whom hadn't had any gum or candy for two or three years, was willing to become a beggar and ask, verbally or by body language, if they could have some chocolate or gum.* They must have wondered and believed that I had at least a taste.

I was sure that the image and memory of candy and gum, the special prize of any child, must have been held tightly in their minds. For years it hadn't been for real, tightly held in their fists or secured in their pockets.

They were so grateful for freedom and our desire to help them with these meager food supplies that they refused to tarnish their feelings of gratitude for something so nonessential and so extravagant. In other places I had served, an American in uniform was fair game on the street for kids with a sweet tooth. It became a conditioned response; a group of kids, their immediate, strong request, hand in the pocket for pre-placed goodies for such an encounter, and the pleasure of dispensing the same. Here there had been no request. Against the Berlin backdrop, the difference was staggering. During my hour with them at the fence, not one had given the slightest indication of his or her thoughts about the desire for gum or candy.

Instinctively I reached in my pocket and found that I was woefully underprepared for such a moment. All I had was two sticks of Wrigley's Doublemint gum.

Thirty kids and two sticks, there will be a fight, I rationalized, making a last ditch attempt to resume my course to the jeep.

That was not a satisfactory answer. Such a little thing, two sticks of gum.

A question came to me. *Will you share it with the kids?*

The issue was time. I glanced over my shoulder. The children were there, even pressed against the barbed wire fence, still waving as is the European custom, until the departed guest disappears down the road.

Now was the moment of truth. To the jeep or back to the fence?

I didn't know it then, but if I chose the fence, my life would never be the same again. My father had taught me that good things would happen if you did something for someone without expecting anything in return. I remembered my lesson when my father had taught me the lesson of the bit of the horse—little things mean a lot!

I turned abruptly and headed for the fence.

Our C-54's lined up to be unloaded at Tempelhof. I took this photo from my airplane, and remember, we were delivering flour, coal and dried food. The C-54 could haul much more food in the dried form. Coal became more important as the brutal winter weather came on.

The Rhein–Mein status board, where the daily tonnage hauled to Berlin was posted, was located on the old brick control tower.

Unloading coal in Berlin.

Hitler's grand Reichstag edifice was a central aiming point for allied bombers. It represented the center point of the destructive forces that Hitler sent upon the world. The gardens, created in the midst of cleared rubble, were a symbol of hope and augmented the dried eggs and dried potatoes airlifted to the Berliners.

The traveling snack bar and the weatherman's jeep at Tempelhof

A British Airman directs the loading of coal in an Air Force C-54 at Fassberg in the British Zone.

I knew my candy ration wouldn't be enough for all the children, so I enlisted the help of my crew. Pictured from left: me, TSgt. Herschel C. Elkins, and Capt. John H. Pickering

Chapter Five: Children of Berlin

Uncle Wiggly Wings

Within the first three return steps the children stopped waving. They expectantly awaited my arrival at the fence. Then they saw my hand come out of my pocket and something, unmistakably, was in it.

An image I took myself on that first day I met those children This is the actual group of children who shared those two sticks of gum

Their interest and intensity of expression changed in a flash. There were some who jockeyed for a better position to discover what I had. My fears began to rise that the pushing would take an ugly turn, but it was too late to turn back.

In the last few steps to the fence I broke the two sticks of gum in half and headed for the children who had been the translators. Their hands were now through the barbed wire. There was no need to await my verbal offer. My actions had already telegraphed my intent and they had accepted.

The four pieces were quickly placed. There was a short gasp as one boy engaged a fence barb in his forearm because of the excitement. In all my experience, including Christmases past, I had never witnessed such an expression of surprise, joy, and sheer pleasure as I beheld in the eyes and faces of those four young people. Nor do I remember seeing such disappointment as was evident in the eyes of those who came so close. The disappointed looks were transitory and tempered by their much more difficult

trials and disappointments over the past months.

There was no fighting or attempts to grab away the prize given to the four who were busy carefully removing the wrapper. No chance could be risked that the smallest piece might fall to the ground.

Just before the end of my sightseeing trip, I promised to drop packets of sweets to a group of children during one of my next flights to Berlin. They would know which plane was mine when I wiggled the wings.

The quiet was broken with a rising babble from the rest. They were requesting a share in the tin foil or the outer wrapper. Strips were torn off and passed around. The recipients' eyes grew large as they smelled the bits of wrapper and recalled better times.

After a brief moment they placed the tiny wrapper in their shirt or trouser pocket as though it were a fifty-dollar bill. There was someone special in their lives who would believe their story if there were some evidence.

I must have been a sight, standing there in wide-mouthed amazement. *What I could do with thirty full sticks of gum! They could have the wrapper and all,* quickly went through my mind.

Immediate thoughts of when I could come back to the fence were answered by: *It will be a long time. You'll be flying without any sleep for twenty-four hours and that can't be repeated soon.*

Just then another C-54 swooped over our heads, across the fence and landed. Two little plumes of white smoke came off the main tires as they touched down on the pierced steel planked runway and squealed up to speed. That plane gave me a sudden flash of inspiration.

Why not drop some gum and even chocolate to these kids out of our airplane the next daylight trip to Berlin? We will have such a flight the next day. This suggestion came to mind so fast it caught me unawares.

You will get in a heap of trouble if you are caught, came a quick and rational response. I was a stickler for flight rules.

This whole blockade is a violation of human rights. Compared to mass starvation, this shouldn't get me any more than a minor court martial, I answered myself.

Why not get permission? My rational side persisted.

You know how long that will take? The airlift will be over by then and it is just a one-time thing; besides, we'll only be about ninety feet in the air, answered my desire.

To my own astonishment and dismay, I found myself in the next moment announcing the plan for all to hear. At first their response was cautiously reserved for fear they had misunderstood. I took the opportunity to add, "I will do this thing only if the persons who catch the packets will share equally with everyone in the group."

"Jawohl! Jawohl! Jawohl!" came from everyone in answer to the requirement to share.

Then the blue-eyed girl was prodded by the others to make a clarification. "They want to know which aircraft you will be flying. Such a small package would be too easily lost, especially if you come late and we have tired by watching all day in vain," she excitedly stammered out while gazing intently into my face. Airplanes were landing every three minutes.

I frowned. There was no way to know what specific plane I would be assigned on any flight, let alone that special one. It would be a four-engine C-54 for sure, but even if I knew which one, there would be no way to identify it from all the rest of the planes coming over the apartment building. Then came another flash of inspiration from my days flying over the farm in Garland, Utah.

Why not wiggle the wings? The thought passed through my mind like a lightning bolt. I remembered back in Utah when I started flying out at Brigham City. I had wanted to show my folks that it was me up there in that shiny airplane. I had previously done a couple of spins over the house but my mom just about fainted because she thought I was going to crash. She was pretty scared. So the next time I flew over our farm, I just wiggled my wings.

That was the answer for letting my parents know I was flying over the farm so long ago, and it was the answer now!

"When I come in from West Germany tomorrow, I'll come over the airfield and wiggle the wings like mad on this big airplane. You'll know that's the one with the goods." I demonstrated to them with my arms outstretched. There didn't seem to be anything more to discuss. Action was clearly the next step. Some suggested I leave and get started.

When I returned to the jeep, the driver asked, "Did you get your pictures, Lieutenant?"

"You bet! Sorry it took so long," I replied with no hint that something else more important had occurred and was about to burst my calm exterior.

A Firm Pact of Secrecy

During the night of attempted sleep after meeting the children, I thought through how I would deliver my promise. The amount of gum and candy we could buy was strictly controlled by a ration card, and there wasn't enough on my card to do justice to the kids. I needed the rations from the other members of my flight crew as well—John Pickering and Herschel Elkins. How would they react to my request, and more particularly to the reason for it?

If we put three rations in one package and lost it, we would lose all. The one package wouldn't be very big, but going 115 miles an hour it could make a big impact if it hit one of the targets too directly. At our altitude the recipients wouldn't have time to duck.

It made some sense to split the drop into three packages. It made even more sense to put a handkerchief parachute on each package to slow the fall and mark the treasure. There was an emergency flare chute right behind the pilot's seat that was within Elkins's reach. He could push it out just as we passed over the roof of the apartment house on the final approach.

That decided, I dozed off just in time to be awakened. "Glad you made it back, Hal," yawned John mater-of-factly. "Have a good trip?"

The sales job on my two buddies was effective because their hearts were as big as usual. "You are going to get us in one big mess of trouble," said John. Elkins cast a similar vote. They forked over their neatly packaged and fragrant rations of chocolate bars and packages of gum. The sight and smell of it, and the thought of the kids, sent a thrill all through me.

A firm pact of utmost secrecy was mutually taken and we were on our way to Berlin. We strained our eyes to catch sight of the kids as we approached Tempelhof at 1500 feet. Sure enough, there they were, all together in a little knot in the middle of the grassy strip in front of the apartment building. They appeared to be scanning the heavens. I rolled in left aileron and fed in a little left rudder. The left wing went down, and I quickly did the same thing to the other side to keep the wings wiggling and the nose straight ahead.

The recognition was instant. That little band literally blew up, waving, jumping, and circling. My bone-tired weariness was gone. The apartment house came under the nose of the airplane in a blur. For an instant the group of kids were visible, still waving, all turned toward the building, faces skyward.

We swung around the pattern, I briefed Elkins again on how he would do it on my signal, and quickly we were on the final approach. The three loaded handkerchiefs were attached to the goodies by strings about fourteen-inches long. The handkerchiefs were folded in a special way, ready to drop. By now the kids were out of sight behind the apartment building.

Excitement and concern for what we were about to do was growing in the cockpit. What if we dropped the packages on top of the apartment building or beyond the barbed-wire fence, onto the runway?

"What if an aircraft waiting for takeoff happens to see the parachutes and get our tail number?" asked John with a frown.

"Give me full flaps and 2400 RPM," I replied. No time to change our minds. We were committed.

"Now, Elkins," I shouted. With a quick thrust he had the little packages out of the flare chute and almost as quickly we were on the runway.

The question on all of our minds was "where did the parachutes land?" We would have to wait for the answer. Unloading seemed to take longer than usual. What results would our impulsive act bring?

Soon we were checked out to make our return flight. In moments we were proceeding down the taxi strip inside the barbed-wire fence, headed for the takeoff position opposite the apartment buildings. As we made the last right turn we could see down the barbed wire all the way to the buildings. There was the answer!

Protruding through the fence were three little parachutes extended by several animated arms attached to three vibrant bodies. The little parachutes were being waved without discrimination at every crew as each aircraft taxied by. Behind the three with the parachutes were the rest of the cheering section with both arms waving above their heads and every jaw working on a prize.

"Guess they got it okay, and it looks shared," beamed John's deep voice.

"Sure does. I must have hit them right on the head," said Elkins proudly.

"Wish they wouldn't wave like that," I added somewhat seriously as I slid back my side cockpit window to give the children a return wave. The long trousers quickly identified the blue-eyed girl. She was radiant!

Several conversations were overheard in the mess hall and base operations between pilots wondering why the kids were making such a fuss on the end of the runway. We renewed our pledge of secrecy.

A week quickly went by. The crowd of kids was noticeably larger and still enthusiastic. When we were able to buy a new week's ration we looked knowingly at each other. On the spot we again pooled our resources, came over Tempelhof, wiggled our wings, caused a celebration, and delivered the goods on target. Another week went by and the group at the end of the runway was now a good-sized crowd. We knew that a lot of kids in the group hadn't received any goodies and we set about to correct the inequity. Every time we wiggled the wings of that airplane we were treated to a remarkable spontaneous demonstration of sheer joy.

Fog and the Mountain of Mail for Me

The third week, everything was blanketed in fog—a forerunner of things to come. The dense fog bank swept up from the south and fell over our West German bases at Rhein-Main and Wiesbaden like a down comforter. We literally took off on the gauges from Rhein-Main to Berlin. By the time we got over Fulda, the weather broadcast said the stuff had blanketed most all of Western Europe.

"Wonder what will be open on our return flight?" asked John. "This stuff is practically zero-zero." This meant that we could see zero feet ahead and zero feet above.

We had to have radar to guide us down and even with radar we didn't try and land under those conditions unless it was an emergency.

The mobile snack bar established by the airlift coordinator, General Tunner, along with the personal service of the weatherman, who provided plane-side forecasts, were welcome additions to operating procedures. In turn, we were to stand right by the aircraft and depart the second the big semi-trucks cleared our tail.

However, on that particular flight of the above-mentioned third week, the weatherman wasn't there. With limited fuel it was essential to know where we had the best chance of getting in upon returning to West Germany. After waiting a few more minutes, I told Pickering I was going to run into Base Operations and see if I could get a quick look at the weather map.

As I came into Base Operations, there was a large planning table just inside that would accommodate extended maps, charts, and flight-planning materials. At the moment it was stacked high with what appeared to be mail.

Some of the waiting children. The thought of them compelled us to do "just one more drop" of candy parachutes.

Strange use for the table, and stranger way to treat mail, I thought as I sidled up for a better look at this unorthodox display.

It only took a glance to freeze me in my tracks. The letters were addressed to "Uncle Wachelflugel (Wiggly Wings)" and "Schokoladen Flieger (Chocolate Flier)," Tempelhof Central Airport, Berlin.

I flew back out the door without the weather but with an even larger burden.

"Holy cow, guys," I blurted out. "There is a whole post office full of mail in there for us!" The three of us

decided not only to lay low for a while but to quit. We had done more than was expected and this was the point to stop.

Just One More Drop

Our resolve to not make any more drops held firm through two ration periods. The crowd was bigger than ever. That meant there were quite a number who hadn't received a sweet surprise.

Again we looked at each other knowingly and Elkins said, "What are you guys doing with your rations these days?" In a moment it was determined that we had all saved our rations for both periods. A short conversation resulted in, "Just one more drop and that is absolutely all."

It took about six overloaded handkerchiefs to handle all the goodies our pooled rations required. We had them on the flight deck ready to drop on the next day trip. The weather was good as we approached Tempelhof. The crowd was easily picked up at a pretty good distance. The reaction to the signaling of the wings was reward enough for the last drop. Elkins, now an expert, called, "Bombs away!" We were soon on the ground and in the unloading process.

Taxiing out for takeoff, the testimony to our proficiency was displayed all along the barbed wire fence. As we nosed the aircraft down the runway and smoothly shoved the throttles to the wall we made a solemn pact that this really was the last of the drops.

LITTLE OPERATION VITTLES

1. TOP LEFT. PPESENT LITTLE VITTLES CHIEF CARRYING CANDY & CHUTES JUST SHIPPED FROM U.S.
2. LOWER LEFT. LT. HALVORSEN ORIGINATOR OF LITTLE VITTLES. GIVING CANDY TO HOSPITALIZED CHILDREN IN BERLIN·
3. TOP RIGHT- CANDY CHUTES COMING OUT OF C 54 ON REGULAR VITTLES RUN.
4. LOWER RIGHT. LITTLE BERLIN RESIDENT IN- SPECTING HER LITTLE VITTLES CATCH.

A "Little Vittles" flyer Capt. Eugene T. Williams put together

Operation Little Vittles

The next day on arrival back at Rhein-Main from Berlin, an officer met our plane. This was not a normal procedure. He immediately informed us that the colonel would like to speak with the pilot. I felt my blood pressure rising. When I went obediently to talk with the colonel, I wasn't kept waiting.

"Halvorsen, what in the world have you been doing?"

"Flying like mad, sir," came my best reply.

"I'm not stupid. What else have you been doing?" came a better question.

Then I knew that he knew. *Oh well,* I thought, *there must be something in the world besides flying.*

"Didn't they teach you in ROTC at Utah State to keep your boss informed?" came a burst. Things looked grim. He reached under the desk and came up with a German newspaper. "Look at this. You almost hit a reporter in the head with a candy bar in Berlin yesterday. He's spread the story all over Europe. The general called me with congratulations and I didn't know anything about it. Why didn't you tell me?"

My reply was rather weak. "I didn't think you would approve it before the airlift was over, sir."

"You mean to tell me that after we had dropped thousands of sticks of bombs on that city and the Russians are now trying to starve the rest of them to death, that you didn't think that I would approve dropping a few sticks of gum?" he asked incredulously.

He informed me that General Tunner wanted to see me and that an International Press Conference had been set up for me in Frankfurt. "Fit them into your schedule," he told me. "And Lieutenant, keep flying, keep dropping, and keep me informed." He smiled for the first time and shook my hand.

I considered it a miracle that six of our large silk parachutes were returned so we could use them again. Eventually that number was reduced to one. This photo was taken in May 1963. The parachute is currently in the a museum at Wright-Patterson Air Force Base in Dayton, Ohio.

I left the office in much better condition than I had entered. Pickering and Elkins were waiting for me. "Are we going to have a new pilot?" Elkins asked. It was a rhetorical question. They already guessed all was well from the look on my face.

Best I could figure, the newspaperman must have got my tail number after the drop the day before and thought he was doing me a favor. His newspaper article had probably saved us and the operation. The press dubbed the project "Operation Little Vittles," taken from the big operation, "Vittles," and the name stuck.

The Miracle of the Returned Silk Parachutes

On our next trip to Berlin, we went into Tempelhof Base with our arms full of bags to pick up the mail from the kids. The Base Commander assigned us two secretaries and a place to call home for the operation. With the secret out, I would come back to my room to find my cot covered with cases of candy bars and chewing gum. Handkerchiefs were often stacked along side the goodies. Since there were no changes in our flight responsibilities, the extra help, plus many other volunteers, was essential and appreciated.

Capt. Donald Kline was able to obtain twelve beautiful silk chutes about three feet in diameter. They would handle a very healthy load.

Looking them over and being short on parachutes, I naturally wanted them back to use again. Most everyone laughed at my idea. "Boys and girls will have those things made into shirts and unmentionables before you get out of town," several said almost in unison.

I had one of our secretaries, Giesela write twelve notes in German that said, "Please return this parachute to any American Military Policeman that you see so it may be used again." Next to it I wrote in English, "Please return this parachute to Tempelhof Base Operations for Operation Little Vittles."

"You'll never see them again," said Lt. Bill Christian, a usually upbeat and optimistic friend. But that afternoon, we watched the crowd celebrating as the larger chutes billowed and serenely sailed on a gentle breeze to different parts of the group. I could even almost hear an "AH!" from below at such a sight.

That afternoon on a subsequent flight, I ran into Operations to see if some might have been returned. My expectations were not very high so it was a double pleasure to find six of the twelve waiting for me. Eventually that group was reduced to one. It is in the Air Force museum at Wright-Patterson Air Force Base, Dayton, Ohio.

Parachute Donations

Operation "Little Vittles" was in full sway. However, in spite of the many donations, we began to run out of parachutes and used old shirt sleeves for candy bags and shirt tails for parachutes.

It didn't take the Berlin children long to hear about our parachute shortage. The letters we received began to include parachutes the kids had caught that were returned for refills. Those who hadn't caught any made parachutes of their own. The parachute usually had a companion piece, most often a map of where to drop it once filled.

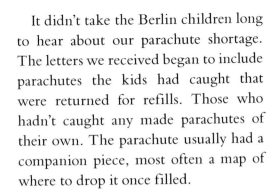

One day I stopped at the mailroom at Rhein-Main hoping for a letter from Alta or the folks. It had been over two weeks without any mail from them. I was taken aback when the mailroom clerk asked me a second time for my name and then my I.D. card. The reason was soon apparent.

The clerk went to the back room and returned with a half bag of stateside mail. "Bring the bag back when you get through, Lieutenant," he said with some wonderment.

My crew and I were on our way back to the barn

Some New York Children receiving instructions on how it is done. September 1948.

LIFE SAVERS
Corporation

Executive Offices and Main Factory

PORT CHESTER, N.Y.

October 21, 1948.

Lt. Dale Halvorsen.
Operation Little Vittles.
Westover Field, Mass.

Dear Lt. Halvorsen:

We have just received a memorandum from Mr. E.E. Anderson, one of our directors, telling us about the very unique brand of thoughtfulness that you are showering on the Berlin children. It goes without saying that generosity as free of provisos and conditions as yours deserves loud applause.

We join all others the world over who have heard of your enterprise and hoping for its continuance. We are pleased to donate our share of this savory jetsam and have therefore arranged to ship you 200 boxes of Life Savers, in all, some 4,000 rolls.

In order that our share of the cargo be distributed at peak freshness, we plan to ship you 1,000 rolls of Life Savers during the next week and follow this up with successive shipment of the same quantity at your request.

Just notify us by card as often as you have cargo space and we will send our product forward within a week of your request. Again, we wish you and "Little Vittles" continued success and assure you of our continued cooperation.

Yours very truly,

LIFE SAVERS Corp.,

John L. Burnett

JBurnett;f   Advertising Department.

IF IT HASN'T A HOLE———IT ISN'T A LIFE SAVER

One of the many mailbags full of envelopes with handkerchiefs for parachutes.

where we stayed, and in a few minutes the mystery was solved. Most of the letters were from the East Coast. All of the envelopes were stuffed with handkerchiefs for parachutes. The wire services had carried reports of shortages and the radio stations up and down the East Coast and from out West were playing tunes if the requester would send handkerchiefs to Operation Little Vittles. The *Weekly Reader* children's magazine also sent parachutes, letters, requests for pen pal names, and addresses from its young subscribers.

We started to receive many dozens of letters, many of them from the East Coast and all of them stuffed with handkerchiefs for parachutes. Many handkerchiefs had the donor's name and address written on them. The wire services had also mentioned that I was a bachelor, which explained the black-laced and perfumed contributions. We dropped them all.

Supplies came in from the Armed Forces troops in West Germany. Contributions arrived from Great Britain and as far away as Australia. The Non-Commissioned Officers' wives club, the Officer's wives club, and the service clubs at Rhein-Main set up assembly lines and handled logistic problems.

Chicopee, Massachusetts had built a new fire station and converted the old one at Grape Street into a 24-hour assembly station for Operation Little Vittles. They became the center for Little Vittles in the United States. Twenty-two schools were organized in full support of making and collecting parachutes, candy, and packaging. They collected 2,000 custom-made shipping cartons, 11,000 yards of ribbon, 2,000 sheets for parachutes, 3,000 individual handkerchiefs, and 18 tons of candy and chewing gum.

At the end of the airlift, twenty tons of chocolate and candy had been dropped by parachute, and three tons delivered on the ground to hospitals, orphanages, and other organizations. Due to the great generosity of so many groups of such variety, a small beginning of two sticks of gum turned into an outpouring of support for freedom and hope.

Dropping Candy in East Berlin

In the beginning of the operation, I was dropping mostly to Western Berlin, the free part of Berlin. However, the kids started writing letters like mad from East Berlin. There was no Berlin Wall up then, so they could travel back and forth from East to West Berlin easily. The kids would write from East Berlin and say, "Look, we can go over to West Berlin and we are catching some of the candy and it's fantastic."

They added, "We like Americans. We can't help it if we are in the Russian Sector. It's just the way it is. One problem we've got is that there are so many people over there in West Berlin chasing the parachutes, we don't do too well. We're not complaining, but we just

On Christmas Eve in 1948, my crew and I were on a flight from Frankfurt to blockaded Berlin. That evening there was a special spirit in my heart that I will never forget, and I was grateful for the opportunity to serve my fellow man.

wondered if when you came over East Berlin if you could drop them over East Berlin." So I did.

We dropped over a number of church yards and recreational parks and playgrounds that we flew over as we came around the pattern of land. I'd pick out areas in East Berlin where the kids were playing and drop to them. Those kids stopped everything to chase the parachutes.

Two weeks later an officer met me at the airplane in West Germany when I returned and said, "Halvorsen what are you doing over East Berlin?"

I said, "I'm dropping to the East Berlin kids just like the West Berlin kids. I don't care what the politics are, kids are kids." He said, "You can't do that."

I said, "Why not? The rules of gravity are the same on both sides of the border!"

"The Russians are complaining to the State Department that it is a capitalist trick and propaganda. The air space over East Berlin is their air space and you can't violate it by dropping things out of an airplane," the officer replied. He said the State Department said I was going to have to stop.

After that, I had to stop dropping in the East, but I believe they were the most appreciative of anybody.

A Special Christmas Eve

On Christmas Eve in 1948, my crew and I were on a flight from Frankfurt to blockaded Berlin. We were one of many crews. Each of us had 20,000 pounds of flour, coal, dried eggs, fresh milk, and medicine for babies. As a special surprise, many chocolate-filled parachutes were ready to be dropped to children all over West Berlin and delivered to the polio and tuberculosis hospitals.

It was a Christmas I will never forget. In my cockpit I thought about other Christmases and felt a deep sense of gratitude that I could be serving just as I was serving at this moment. Giving had become so much more important to me than receiving or acquiring more "things."

I had come to know life's greatest joy—that of "service before self."

Hospital Visits

There was a polio hospital in West Berlin that was full of kids with severely limited mobility. It was visited on a

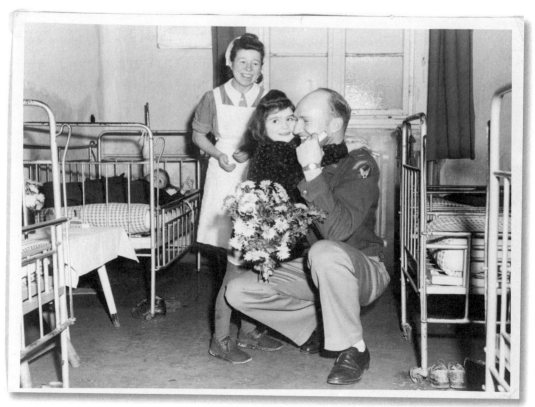

A little girl recovering at the TB and Polio hospital

regular basis by an American health officer, James Gibson, to make sure the children received what they needed from the airlift. On one of his rounds, the doctors handed him a packet of letters from the kids for delivery to me.

The letters were pretty much the same, not an expression of self-pity but an expression of thanks for the daily flights in good and bad weather to support the needs of their beloved city. They went on to mention, almost apologetically, that they were unable to run or walk in an attempt to catch a little parachute.

The main point they all wanted to make was for me to disregard the "Quiet" sign on the streets outside the hospital. The doctors had promised it would be okay to fly low over the hospital and drop the goodies in the yard The doctors would bring the parachutes, with the attachments, to the children's beds.

"We have read about your drops and heard of it on the radio. Every time we hear an airplane close, we hope it could be Uncle Wiggly Wings. Could you try especially for us?" they pleaded.

I gathered up a good supply of Clark and Hershey bars, plenty of bubble gum, and hitchhiked back to Berlin again. James Gibson met me at the aircraft and soon we were at the hospital. Mr. Gibson could really blow bubbles and he taught the children how. The chocolate was really appreciated but the bubble gum was the hit of the day. It wasn't long until we could hear bubbles popping up and down the wards.

If my heart had been full before, it was now overflowing with the reaction and spirit of these marvelous young people who couldn't chase a parachute.

The town of Chicopee, Massachusetts, built a new fire station and converted the old one at Grove Street into a 24-hour assembly station for "Operation Little Vittles."

I was nervous when the officers found out my crew and I had been
dropping candy without permission, but they were very supportive.
After scolding me for not telling him about the first drops, my
commanding officer told me, "Lieutenant, keep flying, keep dropping,
and keep me informed." Thus "Operation Little Vittles" was born.

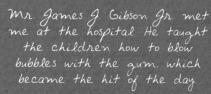

Mr. James J. Gibson Jr. met me at the hospital. He taught the children how to blow bubbles with the gum, which became the hit of the day.

One day, I thought of the three hundred kids in a hospital in Berlin. They all had polio or tuberculosis and couldn't go out and chase a parachute. I gathered up a good supply of chocolate and chewing gum and made my way to the hospital.

Children at the Tempelhof fence, where we dropped candy
the day before. Captain Pickering in the foreground.

The Rhein-Mein Community Center and some of the first volunteers.

Due to the great generosity of so many groups
of such variety, a small beginning of two sticks
of gum turned into an outpouring of support
for freedom and hope.

I heard some children would be on the ramp at Tempelhof, so we didn't drop these until we landed.

I never could have guessed how much Operation Little Vittles
would impact the Berliners. Even before it was an official
operation, letters came by the hundreds. Many included
homemade maps so we could drop directly to a child's home.

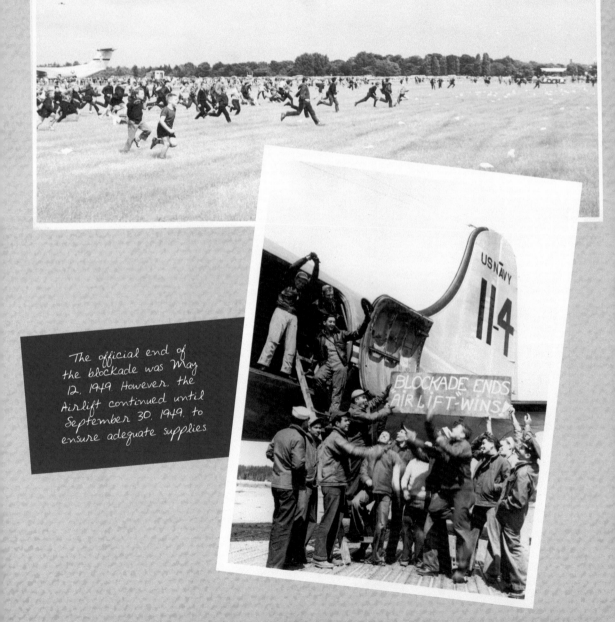

The official end of
the blockade was May
12, 1949. However, the
Airlift continued until
September 30, 1949, to
ensure adequate supplies.

Chapter Six: The Impact of Operation Little Vittles

A Berlin Father's Birthday Gift

I once got a letter from a father who said he had been despondent. He had been trying to whittle a simple present for his son but they had no lights in the apartment. His son had a birthday the next day and there was absolutely nothing special that could be provided to eat or play with.

Dawn was coming and as he stared out the window, he saw something white on the roof outside the window. He got a mop stick and caught the object. It was a handkerchief and suddenly he saw that there was something tied to it. He pulled it in through the window and saw it was carrying candy and gum. He couldn't believe it; he had the best birthday present for his son that he had in the last three years. It was something that couldn't be bought.

The Good Luck Teddy Bear

In 1948, during the Berlin Airlift, groups of school children were allowed to come on the tarmac in organized visits to observe the airlift. One little girl, accompanied by her mother, came to my C-54 as it was being unloaded on the tarmac at Tempelhof. She brought me her most cherished and only surviving possession—a well worn teddy bear that had been her constant companion during the British and American bombing raids and then later when the Russian rockets tore away the last of the city's defenses.

She offered it to me with deep emotion saying, "This kept me safe during the bombings. I want you to have it to keep you and the other fliers safe on your trips to Berlin."

I tried to refuse it but her mother said that I must accept it because her daughter wanted to do all in her power to help save their city.

"Good luck he will bring you and your friends on your flights to Berlin," she said.

This gift meant all the more to me not only because of the obvious love with which it was given, but because it was given without knowing that I was Uncle Wiggly Wings. She had come to present it to any airlift pilot representing all air crews and ground crews. I just happened to be with my aircraft near the terminal. I would never forget my feelings as the little girl curtsied, turned, and waved goodbye.

I put the teddy bear in the windshield of my airplane. Not long afterward, we were flying the C-54 through clouds on our way to Berlin when the clouds abruptly cleared and there we were—

eyeball to eyeball with another C-54 heading the opposite direction!

We barely missed each other on that day. Perhaps we have the little girl and her precious gift to thank.

Mercedes and the Chickens

Even before *Little Vittles* was an official operation, letters came by the hundreds. One of the Berlin letters was from a little girl, Mercedes, seven years old in 1948.

Mercedes Simon lived in an apartment with her mother and maternal grandmother, close to the Tempelhof runway approach. She had lost her father during the war. She and many other children like her were malnourished and underfed. At the time of the airlift, Mercedes's mother was considering sending her away to Switzerland to her aunt's home. The Kinderluftbrücke (Children's Air Lift) was part of the Luftbrücke (Airlift).

When Mercedes heard about the chocolate parachutes coming from the sky, she begged her mother to take her to Tempelhof Airport to try to capture one herself. They went, but were unsuccessful in catching a parachute. She came home sad and discouraged. "Weine nicht, tu etwas!" her grandmother told her.

Mercedes Simon was seven years old at the time of the Airlift. She wrote to me asking if I could drop a parachute near her chicken coop, but I mailed her a package instead. She was nine when this photo was taken.

problem for us. We need the eggs. But when you fly over the garden and see the white chickens, please drop some candy there and all will be ok. I don't care if you scare them.

Your little friend, Mercedes

After Mercedes wrote the letter, she waited in her garden with the chickens, expecting that a parachute would come floating down to her. However, after time went by the weather conditions turned terrible, and Mercedes was about to give up hope. One day she received an envelope in the mail—it contained candy and a letter from the Schokoladenonkel! Here is what it said:

(Don't cry, DO something!). It was then that Mercedes decided to write a letter to her Schokoladenonkel (Chocolate Uncle). This is what the letter said (translated from German):

Dear Chocolate Pilot,

We live near the airfield at Tempelhof, and our chickens think your airplanes are chicken hawks so they become frightened when you fly over to land. They run in the shelter and some molt with no more eggs from them. It is a big

My dear Mercedes,

Thank you for your small letter. Not every day I fly over your home, but surely often. I didn't know that in Hahnelstrasse there lived such a nice little girl. If I could fly a few rounds over Friedenau, I surely would find the garden with the white chickens, but for this there is not enough time. I hope that through what is with this letter, I give you a little joy.

*Your Shokoladenonkel
(Your Chocolate Uncle)
Gail Halvorsen*

After receiving this letter, Mercedes decided to not fly to Switzerland even though she had permission for a flight in one of the C-54s from Berlin to West Germany. She later said that she had hope to get to know her "Schokoladenonkel," and she had a new feeling of protection with her chocolate uncle helping Berlin.

Mercedes remembers, "The sound of the airplanes was standing for the hope of a better future with peace and freedom and good friends. This was the hope of my grandmother, and I trusted in her hope too. Step by step, the chickens were used to the sound of the 'hawks' (airplanes). The chickens began laying eggs again in the summer of 1949 when they had better food too. All these events influenced my whole life. Hope and trust in God are most important things!"[8]

Peter Zimmerman

Another letter I received was from a nine-year old boy named Peter Zimmerman. He sent me several drawings and was quite a good artist. His first letter to me included a crude piece of cloth of about the right size, with four stout strings attached to the four corners. He had not been able to

catch a parachute yet—hence the letter which also included a map.

His map was classic. The letter said that he couldn't run very fast and wasn't doing too well. "Please note the map," he had written. "As you see, after takeoff fly along the big canal to the second highway bridge, turn right one block. I live in the bombed-out house on the corner. I'll be in the back yard every day at 2:00 p.m. Drop it there."

In good weather conditions, the tower would allow me to fly special deliveries after departing Tempelhof and to join outbound traffic when they could fit me in. Most pilots liked to fly low sometimes and I was no exception.

We carefully followed the map to Peter Zimmerman's house. Kids were in the back yard. "Bonbons away!" Next week a letter from Peter came and he said, "Didn't get any gum or candy, a bigger kid beat me to it."

The next try was futile. He continued to send me letters, which always contained pencil sketches of animals or landscape scenes. One picture depicted an aircraft with little parachutes coming out of it. The words, "No chocolate yet," were written on the tail section and suggested his continuing plight. The last

8   Mercedes Simon Wild, interview by Denise Halvorsen Williams, June 2017.

letter didn't have any of these works of art, only:

You are a pilot? I gave you a map. How did you guys win the war anyway?

After that, we gave up trying to drop a parachute to Peter. Instead, I mailed him a package of candy and gum through the West Berlin Post.[9]

In our barracks, we had bags full of German kids' addresses who wanted American pen pals and American kids who wanted German pen pals. The secretaries shuffled the letters and sent them out. Peter drew a family in Palm, Pennsylvania. Peter needed shoes badly, and with winter on its way, he needed boots. He drew his foot on a piece of paper and mailed it to his new pen pals, and in turn they sent him his boots.

Klaus Rickowski

It was a perfectly normal schoolday in the blockade in the morning about 7:30 and I was on my way to school with a few children from Pashener Alley, in Britz. We heard above us the humming of a Rosinen bomber (C–54) and continued talking. We all recognized them, the big silver birds which found their way above

us day and night. We collected pictures of the Dakotas and the Skymasters and built models of them. We were all technicians and we knew all about the airplanes.

Suddenly there was great excitement on our street. Shouting, running and pointing up to the sky. A few little white specks were hovering there. That was something new. I had heard them talking a little bit about the parachutes with the candy and I wondered if that was something like this. I would certainly like to have one of those little things and the wild hunt began.

The parachutes became larger and were coming down over the park in Britz driven by the wind over the area of the Fritz Carson school. The kids were already tearing around through the bushes looking for a parachute. I had two of them in sight and ran in the direction of a park where there was a little pond in the area.

One parachute landed just in front of the pond and was immediately gobbled up by a whole bunch of kids. The other fell right in the pond in the middle of the water. My fear was very short. Throwing off my knapsack and my shoes, in I went. The fact that the water was very cold and dirty and that I was covered up to my armpits with algae and

9   Halvorsen, Gail S., *The Berlin Candy Bomber* (Cedar Fort: Springville, 2017), 118.

THE IMPACT

duck manure and mud was not noticed until much later. More important I had one of the parachutes.

Then came some embarrassed faces. School had long since begun and we were coming late. In my class there were three crumpled up figures who asked the teacher for his pardon. When we had told our story the teacher, who usually was quite strict, was very understanding.

Because I was soaking wet, I was permitted to go straight home.

Even my mother, who was very careful about clothes, which were so hard to get at this time, overlooked the mud and dirt and rejoiced with me.

Sincerely, Klaus Rickowski

Passing the Torch

One day there was a note in the mailbox that several of us were being transferred to Wiesbaden—this meant I was on my way home. One of the first pilots I met there was Captain Eugene T. Williams, a good natured and enthusiastic leader. He had already been one of the outstanding supporters of Operation Little Vittles at Wiesbaden. It wouldn't be long before my rotation date would come up and I was looking for someone to carry on the operation

the way we had it going. Willy sure looked to be the ideal person.

I only had a short time in Wiesbaden to gather my belongings, but I made time to huddle with Willy and another captain, Larry Caskey, about the future of Operation Little Vittles.[10]

Reflections on the Heroes of the Berlin Airlift

In what seemed the next moment, I was at Rhein-Main, a passenger in the back end of a plush C-54 getting ready to depart for Westover Air Force Base at Chicopee, Massachusetts, en route to Mobile, Alabama. Our aircraft turned down the taxiway, revealing the familiar scene of aircraft scattered about the airfield with mechanics huddled about them. Lines of heavily loaded semi-trailer trucks wove in and out of the silver birds like slalom racers, expertly avoiding the flags, homing in on an open cargo door like a magnet latching onto a nail.

My mind went back to the aircraft mechanics. The men were doing what had to be done to breathe life back into the grounded birds. It seemed to me that the aircrews were the ones that got most of the credit in the press and in the

10   Halvorsen, Gail S., *The Berlin Candy Bomber* (Cedar Fort: Springville, 2017), 145.

German communities. To me the real heroes were the aircraft mechanics.

Too often the ground personnel are taken for granted or overlooked in major air events that are outcome centered. Great ones among these are the truck drivers, security policemen, the GCA operators, maintenance personnel, weather people, the communications experts, the traffic controllers, food service and billeting people, the base engineers, the runway repair and construction people, the fire department crews, the medics, the supply workers, personnel people, administrators, operations, and a host of others.

The pilots and ground crew who lost their lives keeping West Berlin alive were heroes who gave the ultimate sacrifice. Besides them, if I had to pick one hero, it would be General William H. Tunner. He was tough, a genius at planning Airlift operations, and truly concerned for the well-being and safety of those called to serve with him.

The overriding heroes and heroines of the airlift had to be the Berliners—men, women and children. Without their knowledge of what freedom meant and their indomitable spirit and principled response, the airlift would have surely failed. They were the ones who went home at night to bomb-damaged rooms without lights, heat, or enough to eat. At the beginning of the blockade the Berliners consciously postponed the return to an easier life for something

better later. They gave meaning to our efforts.

We pulled onto the runway behind a C-54 departing for Tempelhof and in a few minutes we were on our way to Westover Air Force Base in Massachusetts. Before we reached cruising altitude I was sound asleep. My dreams were filled with things long missed, Alta being among them. We had been writing for six years now. I would take a leave out West to see family, friends, and start a new life.

Editor's Note: On November 1, 1999, the airlift/Tanker Association published an article praising Gail S. Halvorsen for starting Operation Little Vittles. The article reads in part:

> *This self-initiated act of kindness became the humanitarian heart that kept the aircrews going, fueled the hope of all Berliners, and set the mold for all future humanitarian airlift. It also provided a catalyst for widespread support throughout the United States for what airlifters were trying to achieve — keep Berlin free from the Soviet yoke. The fame and recognition that followed would open doors for him to serve as a positive "diplomat" to Germany for years to come; a role he humbly accepts without personal compensation to this day.[11]*

---

11   "1999 – Colonel Gail S. Halvorsen, USAF (Ret)," Airlift/Tanker Association, November 1, 1999, https://www.atalink.org/content/1999/11/01/1999-colonel-gail-s-halvorsen-usaf-ret.

First passenger trucks leave Berlin from Hannover May 1949. The sign says, "Hurrah, we are still alive!"

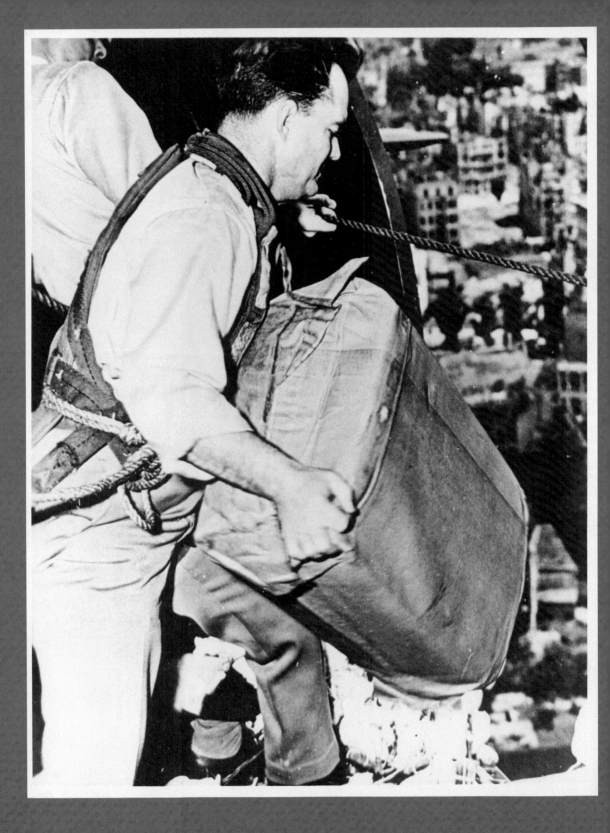

The official end of the blockade was May 12, 1949.
However, the Airlift continued until September
30, 1949, to ensure adequate supplies.

Photo on the left: Capt. Eugene Williams
succeeded me and Caskey. He kept the
project going. He took care of 2,500
different needy children on Berlin's Peacock
Island every two weeks. Willy dropped more
than Caskey and I put together.

The crash of a fully loaded C-47 into already devastated apartments in Berlin. All the crew were killed.

HOW THE AIRLIFT GREW

FLIGHTS TO BERLIN AND TONNAGE CARRIED IN BY COMBINED AIRLIFT UP TO APRIL 3

JULY 1948	AUGUST	SEPTEMBER	OCTOBER	NOVEMBER	DECEMBER	JANUARY 1949	FEBRUARY	MARCH	APRIL
13,520 FLIGHTS	17,925 FLIGHTS	19,494 FLIGHTS	18,235 FLIGHTS	13,574 FLIGHTS	16,405 FLIGHTS	19,766 FLIGHTS	17,006 FLIGHTS	22,163 FLIGHTS	26,026 FLIGHTS
69,000 TONS	119,000 TONS	139,600 TONS	147,600 TONS	113,600 TONS	141,500 TONS	171,900 TONS	152,200 TONS	196,150 TONS	235,363 TONS

Image on the right. In total the Combined Airlift Task Force delivered 2.3 million tons of supplies and made more than 277,000 flights to Berlin during the Airlift.

I never could have guessed how much Operation Little Vittles would impact the Berliners. Even before it was an official operation, letters came by the hundreds. Many included homemade maps so we could drop directly to a child's home.

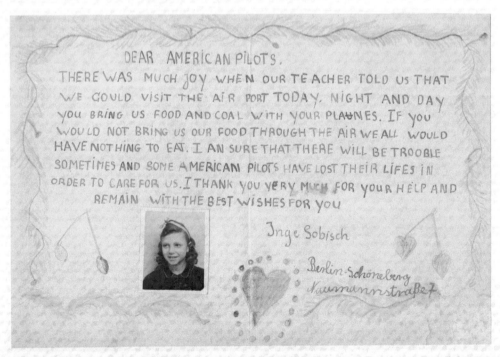

DEAR AMERICAN PILOTS.
THERE WAS MUCH JOY WHEN OUR TEACHER TOLD US THAT
WE COULD VISIT THE AIR PORT TODAY. NIGHT AND DAY
YOU BRING US FOOD AND COAL WITH YOUR PLAUNES. IF YOU
WOULD NOT BRING US OUR FOOD THROUGH THE AIR WE ALL WOULD
HAVE NOTHING TO EAT. I AN SURE THAT THERE WILL BE TROOBLE
SOMETIMES AND SOME AMERICAN PILOTS HAVE LOST THEIR LIFES IN
ORDER TO CARE FOR US. I THANK YOU VERY MUCH FOR YOUR HELP AND
REMAIN WITH THE BEST WISHES FOR YOU

Inge Sobisch

Berlin-Schöneberg
Naumannstraße 7.

My best thanks
for the „Sky-Food".
Rose-Mary Fricke
Berlin-Schöneberg, Gustav-Müller-Platz 1
Berlin, 14^{ts} okt. 1948.

Peter Zimmerman wrote me many letters and was quite a good artist. In this one he wrote: "No chocolate yet," suggesting his continuing plight.

THE BEST WISHES OUT BERLIN FROM
THE CHOCO aroplan at 7ven boys.

BERLIN

FOR THE CHOCO-
MAN.

An artist's conception of a recipient such as young Klaus Rickowski.

A little Berlin girl, Irene Oppermann, who, with
her mother, baked me a gingerbread Santa Claus,
complete with parachute and mock candy bar.

PART 3

THE CANDY BOMBER LEGACY

A visit to the ABC WMOB radio station.

Dad and Mom met me in
Salt Lake City when I came
home in February 1949.

Chapter Seven: After The Berlin Airlift

Post Airlift Celebrations

After my return to the United States in 1949, there were many visits and celebrations. What a reception the town of Chicopee, Massachusetts gave! They were the center of the Little Vittles operation for the United States. Thousands of handkerchiefs made into parachutes during the airlift with candy tied on to them had come from here.

In the words of Andrei Cherny, I was "feted, wined, and dined from the moment [I] landed. [I] traveled all over the country giving speeches of all kinds. [I] sat at tables with dignitaries in Chicago and New York City. [I] spoke at the National Geographic Society in Washington and was given a new sixteen-millimeter Bell and Howell 70DA newsreel camera with three lenses. [I] used this camera for years to record the activities and trips of all [my] family."[12]

No town could take the place of my hometown of Garland, Utah with its 1,500 souls. They had a two-day

12   Cherny, Andrei, *The Candy Bombers: The Untold Story of the Berlin Airlift and America's Finest Hour* (Dutton, 2009), 520.

After my return to the United States, there were many visits and celebrations, including a homecoming candy drop over my hometown of Garland.

celebration, which included permission to fly down Main Street and drop candy out of a Gooney Bird to the kids. They celebrated a special "Welcome Home Lt. Halvorsen Day," where Utah's secretary of state was the guest speaker. I also flew over Salt Lake City and Ogden dropping little parachutes.

Dad and Mom had come up from Stockton, California where they now lived to witness the celebrations. They were pretty proud of their sugar beet thinner. I was still in shock.

Engagement, Marriage, and University of Florida

It took a month and a half from the time I left Germany to get to Alta's home in Boulder City, Nevada. When we saw each other for the first time in nearly three years, and after having written to each other for six years, we both knew that our relationship would continue.

We went skiing up to Mt. Charleston, and when we came down from the mountain I proposed to her and gave her the ring. I had been carrying an unset diamond wrapped in a piece of wax paper in my wallet since I was stationed in Brazil five years before. She said "yes" right away, but I had to convince her I was serious.

Later, Alta would reflect on our engagement, "Once we decided to marry, we just did it. I didn't know how or if our lives would again find a point of alignment if we didn't take this small window. There had been so many other times when we almost got together."

I had thought about marrying her for years, but the uncertainty of the Air Force and what I was going to be doing at the end of the war at first led to me postpone it.

I proposed to Alta in February 1949. The ring is attached to the parachute.

Soon, as an engaged man, I was back in Mobile, Alabama flying the C-74, just as I was before the airlift. Word came that the Air Force was in the final competition for an Oscar at the Academy Awards as the result of a documentary they had put together on the airlift. My Commander asked if I would represent the Air Force at the Academy Awards and gave me two tickets. I said that I'd love to go and I invited Alta. Actress Elizabeth Taylor sat across the aisle from us. I noticed when I looked at people around there that Alta was as good-looking as any of them, but she also had a quality about her none of them had—a graciousness.

Our wedding was on the 16th of April 1949. That Easter Sunday and the bride were the most beautiful sights I had ever seen. Our life together in the Air Force had begun.

She came to Mobile with me, and soon we were transferred to Florida where the Air Force supported my schooling at the University of Florida in earning my bachelor's and then master's degrees in Aeronautical Engineering.

I had to go to Chicago to appear on some programs, the result of my airlift

Alta and I were married on April 16, 1949. The following year on September 16, 1950, our marriage was sealed for eternity in the St George Utah LDS Temple.

experience, and Alta was trapped with the move. She managed just fine, making the move to Florida all by herself. She got all of her worldly belongings in the back seat of a black Mercury car, went to Gainesville, and found a cute little white house in the trees.

After two years of extremely hard work, I graduated with the highest grade point average of anyone in the whole college of engineering, which included the aeronautical, mechanical, electrical, and civil. Then we got a telegram from the Air Force with congratulations and an offer that if I wanted to get a master's degree in aeronautical engineering they would leave us there for one more year. We immediately accepted. We, and I really mean we, graduated with a master's degree in 1952. All this time I was also flying airplanes for the Air Force.

Our first child, Brad, was born while we were in Florida. I was a very happy man and my life and heart were full.

My Work in Research and Development (1952–62)

In 1952, I was assigned to Wright Field in Ohio where I was in charge of Research and Development on advance type cargo aircraft. On Christmas Eve of 1952 our second child, Denise was born, a bright star in our family.

An opportunity came after being at Wright Field only one year to go to Hill Air Force Base in Utah as a Wright Air Development Division Engineering Representative to work on engineering deficiencies that were found in certain aircraft after they got into the operational inventory. Although we knew it might not be the best for my career, we both agreed that we would love to go back to Utah. It had been ten years since I had been West, to be stationed or to live. In the military, I had always been overseas or in the southeast part of the country and I was very homesick to get back into the mountains of the West.

We had to sell the house within one month and it was most difficult because of the old-fashioned nature of the home we lived in. The very last weekend that we were there we were desperate and decided to have a big open house for potential buyers. That day it also happened that my neighbor was in a serious bind to get his corn crop in. He couldn't get any help and I told him that I would help him and left Alta to try and sell the house. I worked all day in the field helping him sow the corn. It happened that one of the people helping in the cornfield talked to me about the house. He lived in the small community, but didn't own his own home. As a result of that contact, and working for our neighbor, we were more than rewarded by the man I met in the fields buying the home the next Monday. He got cash from the savings and loan bank in Ziena, Ohio, and we were on our way.

We were in Utah for four years. I was able to keep flying and do engineering work, hunt, fish, and camp. I was advanced to Major and became the Commanding Officer of element. I could fly about any airplane and I got my first jet flying time there. My favorite was the B26 dive-bomber. Our daughter, Marilyn, was born on Alta's birthday, the 16th of September. Our family was now three of the cutest kids I had ever seen.

From Hill Air Force Base in Kaysville, Utah, we were assigned to the Command and Staff School in Montgomery, Alabama for one full year. The school was very intensive. It was hard work, and went through the summer of 1958. In the summer in Montgomery, Alabama, it is hot and we had no air conditioner. I continued flying here, and flew B25s here and had an engine failure and came in on one engine successfully with no problem.

The greatest event here was the birth of our fourth child, Bob, on Sputnik day—a great addition and the third red head.

After Montgomery, we were assigned to the Space Systems Division of the Air Force Research and Development Command in Inglewood, California. It was the dawning of the space age. I was in the first office that had been set up for that job. This began four years of the most interesting part of my entire Air Force career. As a major in the Air Force, I had unusual responsibilities. I was responsible for the development plan, almost as soon as I got there, to place man in space before the Russians. In September of 1958 the NASA civilian organization was given that responsibility by the government and although I had worked on the space capsules with General Electric and North American and had the development plan written on how soon we could do the job, the task was given to NASA.

I was then given responsibility for the Atlas Booster which was a modified Atlas ICBM to carry the Mercury into orbit. I had that project for some time and then was given the opportunity to choose that one or the TITAN Launch Vehicle modified to make it a space booster to place a manned maneuverable space craft into orbit. I jumped at that chance because I wanted to be on an Air Force program. That involved a man-

maneuverable space craft built like a Delta Wing airplane, revolutionary in technology. It could be placed in orbit and flown back to earth to a landing on a conventional runway. I was responsible for selecting the booster and heading up the engineering team to provide the booster. My studies led to the Titan III, which was the ICBM liquid center core with two strapped on solid booster motors. The glider responsibility was with the Wright Air Development Center where I had served earlier. I worked closely with them and the Boeing Company in bringing this project along. We were not far from launch time, that is within months (1962), when Mr. MacNamara cancelled the program, saying it was too expensive.

I worked in my Air Force career on that concept on and off even later on in the Pentagon. Now it is called the Space Shuttle program and I've seen it land (on television) on a conventional runway as we had advertised. For that effort, I was promoted to Lieutenant Colonel. I gave briefings to the highest levels of the government except the presidential level on many occasions, flying often between Los Angeles and Washington, D.C., to present program plans.

I was also involved in that period in many other exotic space programs: systems to test weapons in outer space,

to put up high reflectors to provide light on the dark side of the earth during certain times. Those were good times, and we loved our opportunity to live in California.

It was while we were there that I heard that there was a chance for a job in Germany in the Research and Development area of technology to determine what the friends and foes were discovering in the field of science and technology in Europe that would contribute to the programs of the Air Force. My boss told me that I was crazy to apply—that this would kill my career, and I had a bright future in research and development. He suggested that I go to the Air Force Base for the launch application and stay close, that I would be promoted much more rapidly.

I believe he was right if our principle priority was how fast we could be promoted in the Air Force, but it was not. Our interest was for the interesting things of life, to see a new land with our kids, to take them to a new land and to be together under those circumstances. So against advice, I accepted a ready offer to go to Wiesbaden, Germany to be involved in discovering all I could about the advancement of science as it might apply to space systems in the European

Theater, including the communist block countries.[13]

Return to Germany (1962-65)

We found a place in Niederwalluf with a German family who had a crystal factory behind their home. It was a wonderful experience, but the most wonderful was the arrival of our fifth child, Mike, at the Wiesbaden Air Force Base hospital, Germany a little over a month after Alta arrived with the rest of the kids from the States.

We lived there for a while and then we were offered a large German house in Buchschlag near the old airfield Rhein-Main that I had flown out of during the airlift times. It was also near the place where the Graff Zeppelin was first launched in a little town called Zeppelinheim.

This was exciting work, but it was mostly secret, and I wasn't able to share very much with the family. They just knew that I traveled quite a bit and didn't talk very much. Here I flew T29 aircrafts and C131s and enjoyed flying very much to the many different parts of Europe.

---

13   Halvorsen, Gail S., *Personal History* (1985), 40–2.

We had such fun family times traveling to many different countries in Europe. It was a remarkable coincidence that Bob, our middle son, was housed in school in the old barn I lived in in 1948 during the airlift. They had built schoolrooms in this old barn and remodeled it and Bob was going to his first grade in the place where I had started the candy drop for the kids in Berlin.

One of our priorities was to get our family to Berlin and show them Tempelhof. I was amazed at the changes that had occurred over the years since 1949. War rubble was all cleaned up. The flight line at Tempelhof seemed to be changed the least. There were a few commercial airliners where the Skymasters had covered the apron. The apartment buildings across the way looked to be in much better shape. For a moment, I closed my eyes and could almost see the kids at the fence.

There were many startling changes to our city of 1949, but none could compare in shock power to the feeling of separation and apprehension instilled by the monstrous Berlin wall. This stark, grey concrete-and-wire barrier to human contact coils its way like a giant snake around Free Berlin. Its only promise was death to those on the other side who would attempt a crossing from East to West. As I stood on the elevated viewing platform at Bernauer Strasse and my eyes swept the death strip, a feeling of darkness swept over me like the accounts of the plague descending. How could this be the 20th century?

Back in the States (1965–68)

We came back to the United States in 1965 and were assigned to the Pentagon in Washington, D.C. I worked there in the Deputy Chief of Staff of Research and Development on man-maneuverable spacecraft, the re-entry from space and many other special programs. We took in all of the cultural advantages of the city and often went to National Geographic Society in Constitution Hall in which I'd lectured in 1949 after coming back from the airlift.

On unexpected occasions, there would be a reunion with someone who had experienced the airlift and subsequent discussion about the world and values in life and the effect the Berlin experience had on us.

One such meeting was with Mae and Ernie Jantzen from New York who invited Alta and I to dinner.

"We've been looking for you for seventeen years," Mae said. "Remember in 1948 when you ran out of parachutes? We heard the announcement over station WOR that they would play tune requests for those who would pledge to send you handkerchiefs for Operation Little Vittles. We sent you three with our names and address on them. In a couple of weeks we received replies from two of the kids who caught them. We have never been able to have children of our own. We informally adopted those kids long distance.

"We sent those kids seventy-seven care packages. When the little girl grew up and got married we sent the wedding dress and when her baby came we sent baby formula. We saved our money through the years, and just two years ago we finally made it to Berlin to meet 'our kids.' She was unable to continue for a moment.

"Those kids have blessed our lives. They were an answer to a prayer, and all for such a little thing as three handkerchiefs! I think it was one of the littlest decisions we've made in our lives, writing our names on three handkerchiefs, but the results have exceeded all the good things that have never happened to us."

"I know, Mae. For two sticks of gum our lives haven't been the same," I said, taking hold of her hand.

One day, while I was in the middle of a design problem in the Pentagon, the phone rang and General Dave Lowe, who I'd worked for in the early space program in Los Angeles, approached me and said, "How would you like to get out of the Pentagon a year early and head up a satellite-tracking facility at Vandenberg, California?" I told him that I'd love to do it.

My new job at Vandenberg Air Force Base was to be commander of the Instrumentation Squadron that helped with the launch of missiles and spacecraft at the tracking station. The station had orbit control of military space satellites around the world. It was the highest priority job the Air Force had at that time in the working of the military satellites. We were guaranteed that we would be there for four years because of the critical nature of the assignment, therefore we bought a house and had it built.

My job was demanding and I was often at the tracking station late at night for a special launch or a special readout on a satellite. Whenever an emergency occurred at the station, I had to go out immediately, so it was a 24-hour a day job.

It was while we were there that the first of about five invitations to return

to Berlin and participate in special ceremonies was offered to us. We got the shrubs and the lawn in and the place was looking beautiful and we were really starting to settle down and then I got a serious invitation to go back to Berlin and participate in the airlift celebration at the annual Tempelhof Open House. Those two sticks of gum were about to change my life once more.

1969 Tempelhof Open House and Parachute Drop

One day the phone rang and the voice said, "Colonel, are you one of the guys that flew the airlift to Berlin? Are you Uncle Wiggly Wings?" I acknowledged the affirmative.

He continued, "Those kids that caught your parachutes in 1948 and 1949 have gone to the Air Force Colonel commanding Tempelhof, Clark Tate, and told him their little kids want to see what it is like to catch those parachutes. The US Air Force still runs Tempelhof just like we did during the airlift. Once a year we open up the airfield to Berliners for two days to show them the cargo planes we have to support the city, if needed, and make a little celebration out of it. We set up a bunch of stands and sell them American ice cream and hamburgers. They love it. Now they

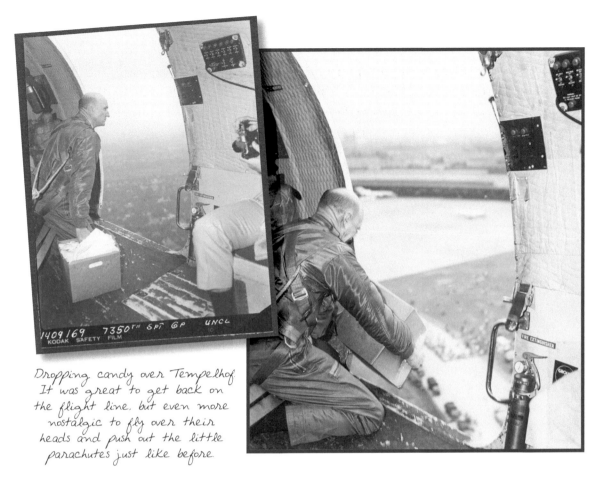

Dropping candy over Tempelhof
It was great to get back on
the flight line, but even more
nostalgic to fly over their
heads and push out the little
parachutes just like before.

want you to come and drop goodies to their kids during that celebration. Will you do it?

Soon I was on my way. I had sent ahead a list of names from old letters and by the time I got there the police had located a lot of the 1948–49 kids who had caught parachutes. They brought their children. We had a big lunch together, exchanged stories, and laughed at the pictures they had sent me in their letters way back then

It was great to get back on the flight line, but even more nostalgic to fly over their heads and push out the little parachutes just like before. The kids ran just as fast as ever. One little American girl, the daughter of a service family, wasn't fast enough to catch any of the parachutes. She was sobbing quietly when a young German boy came over, put his arm around her, and gave her one of his two parachutes filled with candy.

Commander Clark Tate was a great man. That July 1969 trip to Berlin was topped off with a lovely dinner at his

In July 1969, I was invited to return to Berlin to participate in an open house of the Tempelhof Airport and a commemorative candy drop. These were some of the children of the children I dropped parachutes to in 1948 and 1949.

responsibilities that fell on his shoulders and the unusual conditions in which he had to work. Berlin was a very different place from any other Air Force assignment I had seen.

When we pulled up to his house, there was still enough of the farm boy in me to cause a little gasp. The Germans had provided the home for the Commander of Tempelhof since the Americans took over the base from the Russians in 1945. Clark Tate described his job:

"My job isn't limited to running the airfield and the other interests the Air Force has in Berlin. My second hat consists of being the United States Air Force Representative to the city of West Berlin. In that role we are required to host the international community in this house and at the Air Base. We do what we can to further understanding between our Allies and the six American

residence the night before I returned to California. Clark picked me up at the airfield for the ride to his residence in Dahlem for that meal. His vehicle was a Mercedes complete with a professional German driver and communications equipment.

Clark went on to explain that the Germans provided the support required to run the airfield. Some of the finest German employees labored with pride to keep that airfield in top condition.

Although Clark and I were of the same rank, I marveled at the special kinds of

Sector Borough Mayors, their town councils, and the German residents of the American Sector of West Berlin. It may look like a posh job, but don't you ever believe it.

"Don't misunderstand me—I like it—but it sure does put some mileage on you and take you away from your family. There is some official party or function every night somewhere in the city and we're expected to be there. In between there are shootings or incidents at the Wall. I'm on 24-hour call. I've been in a lot of demanding jobs, but none that takes as many hours as this one does. When we're invited, protocol requires that we invite each host back to our place. A lot of our activity is with the British and French officers and men of the airfields at Gatow and Tegel.

"What would you like to drink, Gail? I've got whatever you want. If it is not here it will be in the basement," Clark invited. He went on to explain that the extensive bar was part of what he had to have to fulfill his entertainment responsibilities. "You know that it's simply part of European custom to socialize with the help of alcohol. It's part of their culture and it isn't so different in the United States. I have a bar just as complete in my office on the flight line for guests who visit out there," he stated.

"Thanks, Clark, but could I have a 7-up or an orange juice?" I asked as tough as I could.

"What's the matter, Gail? Do you have ulcers?" asked Clark in a disappointed tone of voice. "No ulcer. I don't drink because of my faith," I replied

"How long is the commander's tour of duty here, Clark?" I asked.

"The longest since 1945 has been two years and eleven months. Don't know if I'll make it that long or not," he answered.

Soon it was time to go, and the big Mercedes and driver were waiting for me at the curb. Clark said, "Give my best wishes to Alta and have a good trip."

"Sure glad I haven't got your job!" I said with sincerity as I headed for the car. "Thank you again."

Once back in California, I told my children all about dropping the parachutes to the children of the children who had caught them in 1948. I told Alta about Colonel Tate and his wife, the big house they lived in, and the difficult and busy job. "I'm sure glad I don't have that job!" I exclaimed to her, shaking my head.

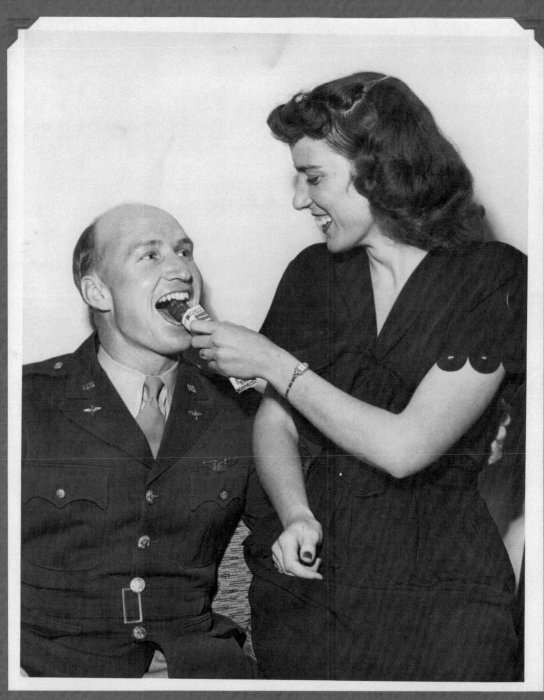

When we saw each other for the first time in nearly three
years, and after having written to each other for six years, we
both knew that our relationship would continue.

I loved meeting people as I signed autographs.

Shaking hands with the Air Force Colonel
commanding Tempelhof, Clark Tate. He
told me how much my visit meant to the
Berliners and thanked me for coming

While I was in town for the candy drop, I
stopped in at a local orphanage to visit with
the children there

In May 1949, I was invited to Washington, D.C. where
General Hoyt S. Vandenberg presented me with the
Cheney Award for my humanitarian actions in 1948.

OAK SAFETY FILM   2

Just before Christmas of 1969, I got a surprise call from Washington, D.C. instructing me to report to Berlin immediately. Tragically, Col. Clark Tate had just been diagnosed with a fatal illness, and General Joseph Holzapple wanted me to take over command of Tempelhof. We arrived on February 12, 1970, in a driving snowstorm, and began a most interesting and demanding four-year period of our lives.

Chapter Eight: The Move To Berlin

The New Commander (1970–74)

Just before Christmas of 1969, the telephone rang and it was Col. Ryan from Washington. He inquired if I had submitted my retirement papers yet, and after hearing my reply in the negative said, "This is notification that you will be assigned overseas in July 1970."

"Wait a minute," I immediately responded with feeling. "I'm on a four-year 'frozen' tour and I've only been here eighteen months."

He told me he was aware of that, but was in charge of assignments in my field. There was a priority request for me personally and the Air Force decided to honor it. He gave me two reasons for the request, saying the tracking station was ahead of schedule, and the Berliners and General Holzapple wanted me to replace Clark Tate when he would rotate the next July.

I answered, "I really care for Berlin and the Berliners, but I don't want that assignment, Col. Ryan. Get someone else who could do a much better job." He answered that he would try and would relay my feelings. The call was almost forgotten until a few days later, when Col. Ryan was on the phone again with the news that whether I wanted to go or not, I would be assigned as the new commander of Tempelhof in July. General Holzapple thought it would be a good idea to have me return to the scene of my Airlift days. He said my recent trip to Berlin to drop the goodies to the kids of the '48 and '49ers in July got the Berliners all fired up. Well, at least we had six months to get ready.

A few more days passed and Col. Ryan called again. This call was very sobering as he told me about Clark Tate's sudden diagnosis of lung cancer and that he was not expected to live much longer. "There has been a change in your orders," he said. "You will report immediately." It was a greater shock to hear of the news of Clark's tragic illness than of our new orders.

It took me a long time until I was able to gather my thoughts and then to express my feelings about the tragedy. Then I said, "There is something you need to know before we report. I am going to call Berlin and have the bar removed from the house."

"I don't know if you can do that; it's part of the job," Col. Ryan replied. "I'll have to call you back."

A few days went by and I told Alta, "Honey, I think we are off the hook." The statement was a little premature. Once again Col. Ryan was on the phone

a few days later. "General Holzapple says he doesn't care what you do with the bar. Get to Berlin."

I turned to Alta and said, "It looks like we are going back to Berlin for an extended stay for those two sticks of gum!" I had already been to Berlin and back as a guest three times for those two sticks and would do the same for many more times after that. We convinced our children it would be a good idea to go, arranged for our house, packed up, and arrived in Berlin in February of 1970. We landed in a driving snowstorm and a military reception, and began a most interesting and demanding four-year period of our lives.

Four Years in Berlin

My new job as Air Force commander at Tempelhof Central Airfield meant that our time was saturated every night and weekend in the entertaining and attending of official functions. We had many experiences with other cultures, all the Allies, the Berliners, and even the Russians. Every year, we held an open house at Tempelhof Airfield and brought in airplanes of all kinds for the Berliners to come and visit. During those two days, Tempelhof was flooded with visitors, and I met many Berliners who had been children during the airlift.

Alta and I invited the children from a local orphanage to visit us in our home one day

The Germans provided this house for the Tempelhof commanders to live in. It was a large, stately home.

Needless to say it was one of the most culturally enriching experiences that we had ever had. We became fast friends with many Berliners and those of other nationalities. We went to many operas and concerts and dined and went to the finest balls as guests of various organization and governments. My work was fulfilling, full of challenge, and often very sensitive. It required personal and family sacrifice.

During the annual Tempelhof Open House days, Tempelhof was flooded with visitors and I met many Berliners who had been children during the Airlift.

During my time there, I planned for my retirement by completing a master's degree in counseling from Wayne State University. It seemed that I might be able to do something in that field when my service in the military was finished.

For Alta, who was raised in Zion National Park, in very humble surroundings, and for a farm boy who was raised without inside plumbing through his senior year in high school, these kinds of things were mind-boggling. The special pageants put on by the French and the British are

something that can never be forgotten and only remembered with the greatest interest and warmth of recollection.

Meeting Mercedes

In 1971, twenty-two years after Mercedes mailed her letter to me, her "Chocolate Uncle," a man named Peter Wild introduced himself to me at one of our Tempelhof Open houses where there were thousands of people. He said his wife's greatest desire was to meet her "Shokoladenonkel" (Chocolate Uncle). Peter told me that Operation Little Vittles meant everything to a child in Berlin and she could not forget me. After that initial meeting, we kept getting an invitation to go to a home for dinner, but we were so busy with many engagements

A visit to the Airlift memorial with Mercedes' family

Now every time I visit Mercedes, which has been many times since our first meeting in 1972, she pulls out my 1948 letter and I write a new message on it.

related to my assignment as Commander that we refused almost all invitations to private homes. Mercedes and her husband, Peter Wild, were sure that one day her "Shokoladenonkel" would accept their invitation and they were not going to give up trying. The invitations came

for a year and a half before we finally accepted.

As my family and I came into their apartment on the 22nd of September, 1972, we didn't know who she was or the story behind the continuous invitations. When we got there, Mercedes went to the china cabinet and pulled out an old letter and handed it to me. It was the letter I had written her in November 1948. It said, "Dear Mercedes, I am sorry I can't find the chickens in the backyard, but I hope this will be alright." She said, "I'm Mercedes, you silly pilot, and I'll show you where the chickens were!" She took me by the hand and in about five steps pointed from the small kitchen balcony down below in the courtyard, "That's where they were."

Now every time I visit Mercedes, which has been many times since our first meeting in 1972, she pulls out the letter and I write a new message on it.

"From small things come that which is great." A life-long friendship resulted from our dinner together.

Leaving Berlin

We had invested ourselves so much in our four years in Berlin. We were busy weekdays and weeknights. It was a relief of a very heavy load to leave Berlin, but it also involved much sadness. After being

Before our return to the United States, Berlin's governing mayor, Klaus Schutz, awarded me the Bundesverdienstkreuz (Order of Merit of the Federal Republic of Germany), the only federal decoration of Germany, for my service as commander.

I completed the four years as commander of Tempelhof in a formal ceremony on February 12, 1974. General David Jones officiated.

THE MOVE TO BERLIN

invested in the people for so long, to just walk off and leave it—we felt empty. We departed Berlin in February of 1974, having survived in a social environment that demanded a free flow of alcohol, which we didn't provide, but gave lots of love instead.

Through Alta, we were successful in fulfilling our ambassadorial role by entertaining the international community in that mansion of a home with good food and friendship and genuine concern for those with whom we served. It was very hard to leave many good friends, but we also knew we would be seeing many of them again. Before leaving, I was awarded the "Order of Merit of the Federal Republic of Germany" (Bundesverdientskreuz), the only federal decoration of Germany, for my service there.

Retirement (1974)

By 1974, I had been in active service for the United States Air Force for thirty-one years and had accumulated about 7,000 flying hours. It was time that we left the military service. We came back from Berlin to Hill Air Force Base. They had given us our choice of where we would be assigned, and for the remaining six months before my retirement I was the special assistant to the Commanding General of the Air Material Air Area. I was able to do several significant projects before I closed down my career at Hill Air Force Base.

We wondered where in the world we would go and where we would live after we got out. Many of us wanted to go back to Santa Maria, California, for we still had our home there, but three of our kids were at Brigham Young University in Provo, Utah, and we thought that at least for two more years they would be there and if we were there it would be wonderful for our family. On that factor alone, we moved to Provo. We found a vacant lot, built a home, and settled in.

On the recommendation of our lifelong friends DeLamar and Mary Jensen, I took a part-time job in the counseling center at BYU and began working on a doctoral degree. I did this until 1976, and then took a full-time job as Assistant Dean of Student Life at BYU until 1986. Dallin Oaks, who then was president of BYU, had interviewed me for the position when I was still in Berlin as commander some years previous to this time.

The C-54 I brought in for a memorial at Tempelhof. The
Berliners named it "The Rosinenbomber" in 1991.

In 1989, the Berlin Luftbrucke (Airlift) Association brought a retired C-54 to Rhein-Main (known today as the Frankfurt Airport) next to the Airlift monument. The monument has several names of fallen Airlift pilots inscribed in its base.

The official end of the blockade was May 12, 1949. However, the Airlift continued until September 30, 1949, to ensure adequate supplies.

Although work kept Alta and I extremely busy, we did our
best to continue to give our children the attention they
needed. Pictured from left to right are Brad, Marilyn,
Mike, Alta, me, Bob, and Denise.

A family trip to the pool

Becoming Tempelhof Commander in 1970. Me with
General Smith (left) and General Holzapple (right)

„Vulpior"

Mit Col. Halvorsen, im Preis der Prominenten Rennstrecke 1.000 M
Yerischorf, 27. 9. 1970

One of the activities I was invited to participate in as commander was chariot racing.

During one of the open houses at Tempelhof, a man named Peter Wild introduced himself to me. He said his wife's greatest desire was to meet her "Shokoladenonkel" (Chocolate Uncle). After that initial meeting, Alta and I kept getting an invitation to the Wild home. When we finally found time to go, imagine my surprise when Peter's wife turned out to be Mercedes Simon, the same little girl who had written me 24 years earlier.

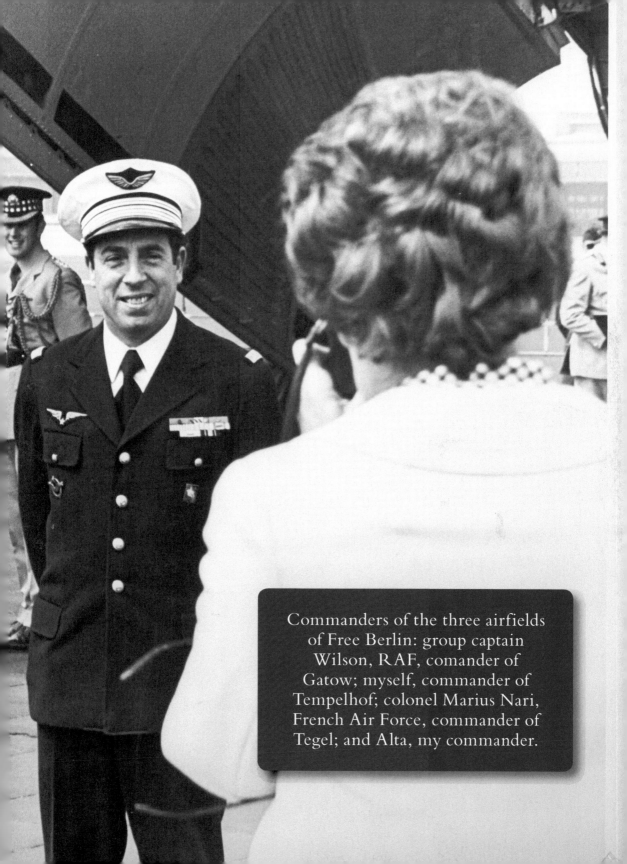

Commanders of the three airfields of Free Berlin: group captain Wilson, RAF, comander of Gatow; myself, commander of Tempelhof; colonel Marius Nari, French Air Force, commander of Tegel; and Alta, my commander.

TEMPELHOF OPEN HOUSE 1971

Sturm auf den Riesenvogel

Attraktion in Tempelhof

Bild

Open House, C-5A Draw Quarter Million Gue.

Der Abend

Gewimmel in Tempelhof

B.Z.

"Galaxy" im Tiefflug über Berlin

MORGENPOST

The Tabulator
U.S. Air Force–Aerospace Power for Peace

US-Luftwaffe meldete gestern Rekordbesuch

200 000 Berliner wollten die "Galaxy" sehen

B.Z.

3 Decades of Airlift Advancement

DER TAGESSPIEGEL

Berlins größte Flugzeugschau

THE BERLIN OBSERVER

Appearance of C-5A 'Galaxy' To Highlight AF Open Hous

Sun, Galaxy Pull Crowd to AF Exhibit in Berlin

240.000 Visitors Pour Into 1971 Tempelhof Open House

The STARS and STRIPES

MORGENPOST

OPEN HOUSE '71

Commander's Open Letter

nacht-depesche

telegraf

The STARS and STRIPES

Good bye "Galaxy"
100 Tonnen gingen in die Luft

Offene Tür für alle Flug-Fans

Views of the Berlin Wall and Checkpoint Charlie

Photo on the left: Every
year we held an open
house at Tempelhof
Airfield and brought in
airplanes of all kinds
for the Berliners to
come and visit.

Taking command of Tempelhof

My new job as commander at Tempelhof Central Airfield meant that
our time was saturated every night and weekend in the entertaining
and attending of official functions. We had many experiences with other
cultures, all the Allies, the Berliners, and even the Russians.

In addition to the
Order of Merit,
Mayor Schutz
gave me and Alta
an etching of
Brandenburg Gate.

Ribbon Cutting at 1973 Tempelhof Open House opening

Celebrating German-American
Friendship Day in 1970.

My desk at
Tempelhof, with a
reminder of why
I'm there.

The photographer John Webbe Hoyt took many military photos during my time as commander, including this one. He said about this particular photo: "Of all the photographs I've ever taken of you, this is my favorite, for it shows the kind of man you really are. In this photo the real you takes over and the difference between you and any other colonel I ever knew, comes out for all to see. This is what the Berliners all saw. Not the uniform—but the human being with the huge heart, that was you."

In 1971, I got to fly in the huge C-5 Galaxy for the Tempelhof Open House. It was a real hit with the Berliners and also sent a message that if the need arose, the USAF could still deliver to Berlin with such a transport airplane as this one!

In Berlin when I was commander at Tempelhof, we lived in Dahlem near the Grünewald—a beautiful woods and forest. Our family often went on bike rides together there. Here we pause in front of the Jagdschloss Grünewald, a former hunting lodge dating from the 16th century, with paintings & artifacts relating to hunting inside. Pictured from left to right are Denise, Mike, myself, Bob, and Marilyn. Alta took the picture.

During those two days, Tempelhof was flooded with visitors and I met many Berliners who had been children during the Airlift.

One of the events
of my family's 1980
visit to Berlin, wa
an air drop of
little parachutes
over Tempelhof
from a Military
Airlift Command
C-130. My sons
Brad and Bob flew
in the airplane
with me. Both son
have been in the
Air Force, and Bo
was an Air Force
pilot at the time

I signed several autographs
during the events.

Chapter Nine:
A Lifetime of Service

Berlin-Utah Student Exchange Program

Since 1980, hundreds of West Berlin students have participated in the new Berlin Airlift, a German-American exchange program. This operation, organized by Peter Wild, Mercedes's husband, and Brent Chambers, a German language teacher from Provo High School, is an important extension of the one of the greatest air relief efforts in history.

40th Anniversary of the Airlift

1989 was the forty-year anniversary of the end of the Berlin Airlift. It was a time to celebrate the breaking of the Soviet blockade in Berlin. I made two trips to Berlin that year, one in May and another in September. The September trip included about two hundred airlift veterans and their partners, which made it a special memory. One of the events was an air drop of little parachutes over Tempelhof from a Military Airlift Command C-130.

All of my children were there to witness this event. What a thrill it was to share this experience with them. Soon after this visit to Berlin, the terrible Berlin wall came down. That was a time for great rejoicing and celebration.

The *Spirit of Freedom*

In 1992, the Berlin Airlift Historical Foundation purchased and renovated a Douglas C-54E Berlin Aircraft support aircraft, the *Spirit of Freedom*. Tim Chopp, a good friend and his crew, keep the "Spirit" up and running. On the outside it is painted in the 1948 colors of the 48th Troop Carrier Squadron with a very large red lightning bolt on both sides of the fuselage. On the inside of the airplane, it is an exhibit hall of Berlin Aircraft history. Historical panels are mounted on the walls, mockups of the types of cargo flown are displayed, a memorial with the pictures of those who lost their lives during the operation are there. Charts and graphs, political background information, and cartoons and display cases with models and memorabilia greet eager school children and adults.

The *Spirit* has made many appearances at airports near schools and at numerous airshows across the United States. Most Decembers, Tim and crew and myself fly it at Kitty Hawk, North Carolina and drop parachutes for kids. Often I get to be the copilot. A highly professional and well-informed volunteer team fly and conduct interior and exterior tours of this exceptional aircraft.

In 1998 Tim Chopp, our crew, and I flew the Spirit of Freedom, a renovated C-54, on a visit to Europe for 69 days of air shows and events to commemorate the 50th year anniversary of the Berlin Airlift. In May we landed at Berlin, "Tempelhof" and what a thrill.

50th Anniversary of the Airlift: 1998 Spirit of Freedom 69-Day European Air Tour

In 1998 Tim Chopp, our crew, and I flew *The Spirit of Freedom* on a visit to Europe for 69 days of air shows and events to commemorate the 50th year anniversary of the Berlin Airlift. On May 5, 1998, the *Spirit* and a professional crew of fifteen waved goodbye to wives and girlfriends. We lined up on the runway at Floyd Bennett Field in New York City and put the throttles to the wall. We were flying across the pond for a tour across Europe that would last sixty-nine days and include twenty-seven airshows.

In the cockpit of the Spirit of Freedom

The greatest thrill of the trip was our arrival over Berlin. Traffic control suggested that we fly over the city low enough so that those Berliners who were there during the blockade could see the aircraft and hear those engines. That sight and sound meant freedom in 1948 and 1949.

The days we were at Tempelhof and Schönefield in Berlin, the *Spirit of Freedom* brought thousands of Berliners through the great airlift exhibit inside her gleaming fuselage. It was immediately evident which Berliners were there during those dark days of 1948–49. Each had a special look about them: elevated emotion and moist eyes. "Thank you for our freedom!" was repeated time after time to each of our crew. The genuine gratitude was overpowering. We were just a few accepting their appreciation on behalf of those pilots and ground crew who gave their lives and the thousands of air and ground personnel, military and civilian, French, British, German, and Americans that made the Airlift work.

A Tribute to Alta and Lorraine

In March 1998, while I was in Europe for celebrations of the 50th Anniversary of the Airlift, I wrote a letter to Alta just months before her death. "In thirty-seven days it will be forty-nine years since we exchanged wedding vows and started a journey together through the earthly phase of our eternal journey. I can't imagine how heaven could be better (except for the Savior's presence), than what you have made for me on this earth. You have shared your love for life and those about you completely. I, with our children and grandchildren, have been the lucky special beneficiaries. You have given so much more to every facet of my life than I could ever have imagined that it is impossible to adequately express. You are the light of

After Alta's death, Lorraine Pace and I married. We had dated during my senior year of high school in Garland, Utah, and she had also lost her husband.

We had many enjoyable times together and appreciate many of the same kinds of activities.

my life and a true disciple of our Savior's example of love. I love you. Whatever I have accomplished that is good I owe to you".

I did not know that before a year would pass, Alta would be gone. Her passing in January 1999 left me desolate (Denise Williams, *Alta Jolley*).

After Alta's death, Lorraine Pace and I married. We had dated during my senior year of high school in Garland, Utah and she had also lost her husband. We started a new life together and she

has kept me alive. We have had many enjoyable times together and appreciate many of the same kinds of activities.

Without Hope, the Soul Dies

Over the years, I have met countless individuals and their loved ones who benefitted from the labors of those who took part in the Berlin Airlift. One particular event stands out and it happened during our *Spirit of Freedom* 1998 European Air Show tour in Berlin.

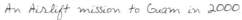

An Airlift mission to Guam in 2000.

I will never forget meeting a sixty-year-old man who came up and spoke to me. He told me he had caught a parachute in 1948 with a fresh Hershey candy bar attached.

He said, "Fifty years ago I was a boy of ten going to school in Berlin. The clouds were very low. It was raining. I could hear the planes landing and taking off. I couldn't see them. Suddenly out of the clouds a parachute with a fresh Hershey candy bar landed right at my feet. It took me a week to eat that candy bar. I hid it day and night. But the chocolate was not the most important thing. The most important thing was that someone in America knew I was in trouble and someone cared." He paused and said with moist eyes, "I can live on thin rations but not without hope. Without hope the soul dies."

Hope is what the British, French and American Airlift, its flour, dried eggs, dried potatoes, dried milk and coal meant to the Berliners—hope for freedom. Everyone needs hope today as much as the West Berliners needed it then.

Hope Is the Name of the Game

Since then, I have flown on airlift and candy drops to children in Yugoslavia, Albania, Guam, and many parts of the United States. Some of my favorite activities have been to visit schools and talk to children about the Berlin Airlift and those thirty children who did not beg for candy and chocolate, but who expressed their desire for freedom above all else. Hope for freedom is still the name of the game. As I look back I thank the blockaded children in Berlin for reminding me of the importance of putting principle before pleasure when faced with an important decision.

Freedom later was more important to them than the offer of food from the Soviets, the joy of food immediately. The Berlin children taught me to be more grateful for whatever I have, but most especially for freedom. The rewards of service to the less fortunate can hardly be equaled.

Gail after a flight in 2017.

Members of the basketball team at the Halvorsen Schule in Berlin encircle Gail at his visit to the school in November 2016.

Talking with the local media

The children, as always, ran to catch the candy chutes.

These dear friends of the Frankfurt Luftbrücke Association sacrifice much to educate and support the memory of the Berlin Airlift through education and service. Left to right: myself, René Paddock, Celeste Warner Heymann, Charlie and Christina Pieroth.

Charlie Pieroth of the Frankfurt Luftbrücke Association helps Gail prepare for the evening of the 70th anniversary of C.A.R.E.

In 1998 Tim Chopp, our crew, and I flew the Spirit of Freedom,
a renovated C-54, on a visit to Europe for 69 days of air shows and
events to commemorate the 50th year anniversary of the Berlin
Airlift. On May 5th, 1998, the Spirit and a professional crew of
fifteen waved goodbye to wives and girlfriends.

Pope AFB crew:
Aircraft
Commander Capt.
Bryan White is
on the back row,
third from the
left. The navigator
is on his left.

As I walked along the flight line at Tempelhof, I couldn't help but think of the Airlift and everything that had happened to me since then.

Holding girl from Berlin with an American Flag in her hand.

"Thank you for our freedom!" was repeated time after time to each of our crew.

50th Anniversary of the Airlift: 1998 *Spirit of Freedom* 69-Day European Air Tour.

On May 14, 1998, Berlin Mayor Deipgen, Chancellor Kohl, and President Clinton christened a brand new C-17 transport *The Spirit of Berlin*.

This special Airlift stamp was also unveiled during our European air tour
The Berlin Air lift commemorative stamp of Templehof 1998.

EUROPE TOUR 1998
69 DAYS

Our 69-day air tour of Europe
included 27 air shows
A memento signed by the crew.

Looking out plane window over the southern tip of
Greenland during our 69-day air tour of Europe.

Tim Chopp tries to keep
warm in the cockpit
of the Spirit after the
heater went out.

Pictured from left to right are Mir Space Station Commander, Major Yuri Gidzenko and NASA astronaut Col. William McArthur. My parachute is in the middle. Two Russian stamps are on the lower left of the parachute.

Out of the C-54 To Berlin children, 1948 —
Out of SPACE, 1995 IN MEMORY OF
THOSE WHO DIED FOR FREEDOM.
                    FROM
                Gail S. Halvorsen
                COL USAF (RET)
                Berlin candy Bomber

Flown in Space 899-74/895-20
From the beginning of the
Cold War to the end. This parachute
we there. Bill McClutters
COL US Army
Astronaut

the

COURTESY:
    KNECT'S
    JOHNSON'S
    NASA
    ARMY AV. DET

Bill McArthur wrote on the parachute. lower
left. "From the beginning of the Cold War to
the end—this parachute was there."

Signing autographs in the Rosinen Bomber in May 1987.

Photo on the left: Flack jackets on. Going on oxygen ready to depressurize. Halvorsen, left, and Maj. Rory Gardner, right.

Gail and Lorraine Halvorsen with President George Bush Sr. at the grand opening of the American Embassy in Berlin. July 4, 2008.

Camp Hope
in Albania 1999

TWO STICKS OF GUM

Two sticks of gum is all it took,
Handed out as engines roared and the ground shook.
They were split many ways, and wrappers too,
So that some could smell while others chew.
Two sticks of gum put a mind to a test,
Of ways to deliver, which one was best?
How would they know? How could he show?
Wiggle his wings? That may be the way to go!
From two sticks of gum and some chocolate too,
Dropped from the skies by those who flew.
It promised a hope that would not be forgot,
Along with freedom that was to be their lot.
They still remember the missions flown,
The tiny parachutes they kept for their own.
That liberty and freedom did prevail.
Hope kept alive by two sticks of gum –
from a man named – Gail.

Dedicated to the Berlin Candy Bomber –
    Gail Halvorsen

Fred "Joe" Hall
Berlin Airlift Veteran

EPILOGUE

The story of the Berlin Candy Bomber and his love for freedom is powerful. Gail Halvorsen's story continues to touch lives and teach the eternal principles of attitude, gratitude, service before self, and the importance of little decisions that set us on the path of life. He emulates the values of kindness and a positive view of life to children and adults all over the world today.

APPENDIX

Gail's Dead Sea Saying

I have learned that giving service to others brings genuine fulfillment. The Dead Sea is dead because it wraps its arms around the sea and does not allow anything out or give anything away.

In man's search for fulfillment and happiness, material rewards pale compared to the importance of gratitude, integrity, and service before self. Gratitude brings unexpected special blessings, communication is facilitated, understanding is accomplished, and progress is accelerated. Gratitude, integrity, and service to the unfortunate provide more rewards than all things material. These principles are the foundation upon which hope is born. They provide the strength by which hope endures.

The thirty-one Americans and the thirty-nine British pilots and crew members who gave their lives to deliver freedom and democracy to a former enemy during the Berlin Airlift gave the ultimate sacrifice to serve a former enemy. Service to others before self was their mission. It is the only true recipe by which full fulfillment may be attained in this life.

Lessons Learned from the Best Teachers

Written in 2013 by Gail S. Halvorsen

1. The desire for freedom is inborn in every human soul, no matter on which side of the border he or she is born. When helped too much, "I do it myself!" comes in every language from the lips of most children when

they are two- or three-years old. Free agency is already at work, but not all are free to choose.

2. Children hold the future of the whole world in their hands; our children and everyone's children.

3. Keep your word. Integrity begets hope, faith and peace of mind for you and others. A West Berliner recipient of a chocolate bar once told me, "Without hope the soul dies." His hope and faith were based on the belief that the British, French and Americans would stand by him and someone in America cared.

4. Give service to others if you seek genuine fulfillment. A happy person has goals that include others. Those devoid of service are wandering Dead Sea souls. No charity here.

5. Be grateful to others with words, service or goods and without preconditions. Unexpected blessings and rewards will be yours. More important, another person's burden will be made lighter.

6. Seek a positive outlook on life and the world will be manageable, even if difficult. Attitude is not everything but it does affect everything. How you complete the mission and in the world of work attitude determines your success or failure. It is more important than grade point average.

7. Little decisions put your footsteps on the path that will lead you to your final destination, good or bad.

8. It is never so good or never so bad that the existing situation can not be improved with patience, determination, love and hard work.

9. My mother always said, "Perseverance wins!" She was right. Patience and work are again the keys.

10. A good woman is uniquely powerful and inspirational. She is to be honored and prized.

11. My father taught that we should not only endure to the end, but also strive to excel through the journey.

12. Families that work together and pray together are the ideal building blocks for a beneficial society.

13. My scoutmaster said, "Always do your best!" He was right.

14. If there is a conflict when you make a decision—put principle before pleasure. The Berlin kids did. Freedom, sometime in the dim future, was more important than the pleasure of enough to eat now.

15. As you travel the road of life look in the rear view mirror to learn but do not look too long for the what if, what might have been, or how great or bad you were, or how bad someone else was. If you dwell too long on these things you will surely miss the turn off on the road to what you might become. Look forward through the windshield for the good in the world and how you can make it better.

16. Similarly we all have mental and physical "mountains" to climb. Part way up you may become weary with the struggle and discouraged. Pause for a moment. Look back and take heart from the good and how far you have come. On the morrow look up. Resume the climb with new determination and confidence.

17. God is alive and well. We plan our challenging journey toward our desired objective on this space ship "Earth." He has given us a GPS that will direct us around the pitfalls of life and radar that we may not ice our wings, or hit rocks in that which clouds our vision. If we keep our batteries properly charged we will make the journey safely back to Him.

Honors and Awards

Gail has received numerous awards and recognition for his humanitarian service. These below represent only a sampling of such. One of his most prized awards is the German Service Cross to Order of Merit of the Federal Republic of Germany (Bundesverdienstkreuz), awarded him in 1974 for his service as Air Force Commander in Berlin.

Gail's autobiography, *The Berlin Candy Bomber,* is now in it's fourth printing.

Dining halls, plazas, schools, and the Halvorsen Loader have been named after him. Musicals and plays are performed at schools depicting the Airlift and the role of the Candy Bomber.

More recently, in 2013, the Alfred Wegnere School in Berlin held a ceremony to change its name to honor Gail. It is now the Gail S. Halvorsen Schule. He was awarded an honorary Doctor of Human Letters degree from Chapman University for his lifetime of service. In 2012, he was given a humanitarian award from the Institute for German-American Relations.

Also in 2012, the story of the Berlin Candy Bomber was the subject for the script for the Mormon Tabernacle Choir's Christmas Concert with Tom Brokaw. Gail appeared as part of the program, and thousands of parachutes were dropped from the ceiling of the LDS Conference center. In 2014 he was featured in the LDS Church documentary "Meet the Mormons."

In 2014, he received the Lufthansa Airline Lifetime Achievement Award and a US Congressional Gold Medal. He was awarded the Wright Brothers Master Pilot Award from the Federal Aviation Administration in 2015 and the Lucius D. Clay Medal from the Federation of German-American Clubs. In 2016, Gail received the Kiddie Hawk Children's Award from the Kiddie Hawk Air Academy at the Living Legends of Aviation Awards, and Lifetime Membership in the CARE organization of Luxembourg.

In 2017, he was recognized in the Utah Senate for his humanitarian service. He was awarded a Lifetime Achievement Hero Award from the American Red Cross.

In addition to these many honors, he continues to receive countless letters and emails from children and adults, both German and American, from around the world telling him how his story has affected their lives. Students contact him to write reports on the Berlin Airlift for school, and talk to him about what they have learned in school about the Airlift.

He is living history. Schoolteachers and students have written to invite him to visit after learning his story. He has made visits to schools to talk with the children, share his books, and drop chocolate-laden parachutes from airplanes and helicopters. Children learn history through the story

In 1977, I was invited back to Berlin to participate in a Tempelhof open house.

It is a joy to me to meet many who remember the airlift and who have taught children about those difficult times.

Receiving the
Congressional
Gold Medal for
Civil Air Patrol
(CAP) in 2014.

Berlin 2016
Halvorsen Schule visit.

Halvorsen Schule visit. Berlin 2016

Mr. Gail S. Halvor

At the Halvorsen Schule in Berlin 2016

At Spanish Fork Airport, left to right: Jim Stewart of the Gail S. Halvorsen Education Center and Foundation, Gail Halvorsen, Bradford Brown (owner), Paul Jensen, and Bob Halvorsen (Gail's second son), 2017.

Receiving the Red Cross award in 2017

Candy drop with Jim Stewart in the helicopter. 2017.

In the helicopter preparing to take off for a candy drop

The drop was a huge success!

Gail and Governor Herbert, 2017.

2017 Salt Lake City, Utah
Gail and family in Governor Herbert's office following Resolution
S.C.R.4. in the Utah State Legislature.

Gail and his children in 2017.

NEARER, MY GOD, TO THEE

 oaring through the clouds
I half expect here to see
An angel dining next to me.
A table here, a table there,
or perhaps a place for a rocking chair.

GAIL S. HALVORSEN

Written in Natal Brazil in 1946
after flying a Douglas Dauntless,
A-24 dive bomber through the
beautiful clouds over the nearby
ocean. Describes my love for the
creations of the "Father" of us all
and my love of flying.

This room is furnished and replete.
The floor is soft for angels' feet.
You've seen the shows and the carpets lined
With a film of cloud that trails behind.

This is it, and first hand now
You see the light in the marbled hall.
The doors are wispy, never slam.
They haven't yet replaced a jam.

For pictures you may raise a call.
but watch those rainbows on the wall.
They change around and hang on straight,
No worry of plaster or adhesive tape.

The Maker of all this must be near,
Some greater presence calms my fears.
How insignificant this machine and man,
In such a great and marvelous plan.

I leave the room, now down the street,
The angels at this lamp post meet
to talk and laugh and play around,
You'd think that life was on the ground,

Till high and free you wandered loose
To watch the spires and taunt the goose,
To feel the breeze and taste the air
That stars and years have heaped up there.

To turn the earth upon it's side,
Then put the nose down in a dive,
To put the gear against the clouds
And leave the heights within their shrouds
That another day may come
And the ascent up once more begun.

*Until that day when He will call
And install the wings that never stall!*

Gail S. Halvorsen

AUTHORS
Gail S. Halvorsen
&
Denise H. Williams